Fasting for God

*Inspiring Quotations on Self-restraint,
Mindfulness & Spiritual Awareness*

Mario A. S. Ahmad

Editor

Writers' Inc. International
Beltsville, MD

Fasting for God:
Inspiring Quotations on Self-restraint, Mindfulness & Spiritual Awareness

First Edition

Library of Congress Control Number: 2019952449

CONTENTS

PROLOGUE

Fasting is to reaffirm to oneself what Jesus answered Satan when he tempted him at the end of his 40 days of fasting in the wilderness: "Man shall not live by bread alone but by every word that proceeds from the mouth of God" (Mt 4:4)... [POPE JOHN PAUL II].

This compilation of quotes on fasting is intended as a stimulus for intercultural dialogue on a practice as old as religion itself. It may also serve as a tool for academic research and study.

This book does not propagate theological doctrines authoritative to any religion, nor does it endorse health remedies or dietary therapies. While advocating interfaith dialogue, it doesn't promote religious syncretism or eclecticism, or try to make anyone a vegetarian, eat kosher food, fast Ramadan or observe Lent.

Further, this is not a how-to-fast book. Fasting is a spiritual practice in all the major religions. To explain the details of how to fast would intrude into the domain of theological creeds and dogma.

While extolling the motivational aspects of fasting, we must also note its limitations. Food deprivation is not for the sick, weak or injured. We need nourishment to regain our health during and after an illness, injury or surgery.

Nevertheless, fasting is more than mere food deprivation. When health conditions prevent restricting our diet, we can choose to restrain other sources of self-gratification, including our listening, viewing and social habits.

And whoever does more good than he is bound to do does good unto himself thereby; for to fast is to do good unto yourselves - if you but knew it. [QURAN 2:184].

INTRODUCTION

Oh you who have attained to faith, fasting is prescribed for you as it was prescribed for those before you so that you may remain conscious of the Divine. [QUR'AN 2:183].

Fasting is usually defined as voluntary deprivation of food, drink, or both, for a limited time. Theologically, food deprivation and other forms of abstinence are often associated with penance, atonement, and purification.

The Scriptures of Hindus, Jews, Christians and Muslims all command or recommend fasting as a religious practice. The Buddhist's "middle way," is best described as guarded eating, a restrained path between extreme asceticism and depraved gluttony,

These religious railings, fences, and boundaries imposed upon adherents are meant to be restraining barriers that seek to guide toward an ultimate reward. They prescribe duties and rituals that test and prove our commitment. They are external, communal practices that may be obligatory or invitational.

Seeking to facilitate our encounter with the Divine, religions establish doctrines and canons to regulate how, when and if to fast. But, fasting goes far beyond rituals and mere food deprivation.

Now it has been stated above that fasting is useful as atoning for and preventing sin, and as raising the mind to spiritual things. ... Wherefore fasting in general is a matter of precept of the natural law, while the fixing of the time and manner of fasting ... is a matter of precept of positive law established by ecclesiastical authority: the latter is the Church fast, the former is the fast prescribed by nature. [THOMAS AQUINAS, SUMMA THEOLOGICA].

A Friend of God

Whether for penance, purification or atonement, invitational or obligatory, the renunciation of physical pleasures is found in every culture and religion. It is a fundamental tool of human communion with the Transcendent.

Privately, fasting is a pilgrimage into a spiritual state hollowed within ourselves. When we fast, we travel to an inner dimension where the great religious masters have also gone to find insight and awareness of God.

> *Today, especially in affluent societies, St. Augustine's warning is more timely than ever: 'Enter again into yourself.' Yes, we must enter again into ourselves, if we want to find ourselves. Not only our spiritual life is at stake, but indeed, our personal, family and social equilibrium, itself.* [PENITENTIAL FASTING IS THERAPY FOR THE SOUL].

Something in the process of fasting elevates our consciousness, carrying us into a closer relationship with the Divine. It is a spiritual exercise that provides extraordinarily satisfying encounters with sacred reality.

The Sanskrit word for fasting, upvaas, literally means sitting near or close to God. As the early Christian author, Tertullian, noted, if practiced with the right intention, fasting makes one "a friend of God."

Fasting Is an Attitude

At times, we may personally choose to deny our desires or forgo pleasures, seeking greater spiritual awareness and a better understanding of our existence. Jesus' words affirm such spiritual austerity:

> *If any want to become my followers, let them deny themselves and take up their cross and follow me.* [MATTHEW 16:24].

From this perspective, fasting becomes an attitude, a way of looking at ourselves and at the world. It presupposes that, with Divine help, we can cultivate willpower and self-mastery to overcome instincts, habits and self-gratifying cravings.

> *But that there may be no error in the name, let us define what fasting is; for we do not understand by it simply a restrained and sparing use of food, but something else. The life of the pious should be tempered with frugality and sobriety, so as to exhibit ... a kind of fasting during the whole course of life. [INSTITUTES OF THE CHRISTIAN RELIGION, CH. 12.18].*

Spiritual Exercises

Embarking on a journey toward God-consciousness requires discipline and self-control. As a devotional leash, fasting begins to check and regulate our gluttonous cravings for carnal, mental and even spiritual indulgences. We tie this leash around our senses and through our intellect, then resolutely hold on to it with our faith.

> *A man who eats too much cannot strive against laziness, while a gluttonous and idle man will never be able to contend with sexual lust. Therefore, according to all moral teachings, the effort towards self-control commences with a struggle against the lust of gluttony—commences with fasting. [LEO TOLSTOY, THE FIRST STEP, THE WORKS OF LEO TOLSTOY].*

However, fasting is just one of several spiritual disciplines or exercises designed to enhance Divine awareness. The etymology of fasting connotes holding back or restraining. This can refer to any passion or appetite which interferes with our piety and devoutness.

> *For as strolling, walking and running are bodily exercises, so every way of preparing and disposing the soul to rid itself of all the disordered tendencies, and, after it is rid, to seek and find the Divine Will as to the management of one's life for the salvation of the soul, is called a Spiritual Exercise. [SPIRITUAL EXERCISES OF ST. IGNATIUS OF LOYOLA].*

Timeless Worship

Acts of self-denial are uniquely accurate replications of timeless forms of worship. Whenever or wherever we restrain ourselves, we all confront similar psychological trials, and experience similar human conditions.

We may not know the exact contents of ancient spiritual rituals, but by simply controlling our cravings, we can feel confident that we are following the path of those human beings whom we most respect and revere.

Divine unity implies a common thread connecting all believers. Though our creeds and dogmas differ, often irreconcilably, our mystical bond recognizes spiritual emotions and awareness that we all share and transmit. It is noteworthy that though the quotations in this book are listed by denominations, they are all infused with the same devotional sanctity.

> *[There is an] outlook which is common to all those who have elected to question the value of life submitted entirely to arbitrary secular presuppositions, dictated by social conventions, and dedicated to the pursuit of temporal satisfactions. [THE WAY OF CHUANG TZU, THOMAS MERTON, IN NOTE TO THE READER.*

1

JUDAIC SOURCES

1.1 Fasting in Judaism

Food prohibition and restrictions in the Old Testament flows from a stream that springs in the Garden of Eden, then flows through the fasting of Moses on Mt. Sinai, into the command for affliction on the Day of Atonement, and the dietary restrictions, *kashrut*, of the Torah.

Yom Kippur, the Day of Atonement, is probably the most revered day of the Jewish calendar. Even Jews who do not normally observe other religious practices will fast and attend the synagogue on Yom Kippur.

Eating and drinking are prohibited for a 25-hour period that begins before sunset of the evening before the day of Yom Kippur, and continues until after nightfall of the holy day.

In commanding the fast, the Torah does not specifically use the Hebrew root word for fasting, tsom (צוֹם). It uses the Hebrew word *anah*, (עָנָה) meaning "to afflict or deny oneself."

Way of Life

Additionally, Jewish spiritual disciplines are based on the Torah's commandments (*mitzvot*), usually enumerated as 613. These commandments, along with later Talmudic and rabbinic writings, customs and traditions form the Halacha, the Jewish law. The Halacha establishes spiritual direction for every aspect of life, thereby molding the

Jewish individual and communal identity. [See *Maimonides' (Rambam)* MISHNEH TORAH].

Being an observant Jew means that you live by an established set of laws and traditions, including daily prayers (*amidah*), dietary regulations of *kashrut* (kosher), holiday observances, and maintaining your home according to set rules.

Spiritual Community

The observance of holidays requires fasting during two major fast days and four minor fast days that are part of the Jewish year. The two major fasts, Yom Kippur and Tisha B'Av, begin before sundown and end after the next sundown, during which Jews may not eat or drink, brush their teeth, comb their hair, or bathe. For the minor fasts, no food or drink is taken from dawn until nightfall.

Every *Shabbat*, the seventh day of the Jewish week, is a day of rest, remembrance and pious observance established by the Fourth Commandment: "Observe the Sabbath day to sanctify it." [Deuteronomy 5:12]. Jews chant from the Psalms, say prayers and recite the "Shema Yisrael," all designed to build *kavannah*, the directing of the heart to higher contemplative thoughts and inner strength.

Study of the Torah

Perhaps the most elevated spiritual discipline for a Jew is *Torah Lishmah*, the diligent study of the Torah.

Rabbi Meir said: anyone who engages in 'lishma' merits many things .... He is called 'friend' and 'beloved,' he loves G-d, he loves man, he brings joy to G-d, he brings joy to man. It [the Torah] clothes him in humility and fear. It enables him to be righteous, pious, upright, and faithful. It distances him from sin and brings him to merit . . . It reveals to him the secrets of the Torah . . . He becomes modest, slow to anger, and forgiving of the wrongs done to him. It makes him great and exalted above all of creation. [[PIRKEI AVOS CH.6 IN TEXTUALITY AND THE BIBLE]]

Jewish Mysticism

In Kabbalah, the mystical tradition of Judaism, esoteric and ascetic practices abound. Kabbalists believe that immersion in its mystical doctrines and practices provides profound insights into Jewish sacred texts and brings them spiritually closer to God.

By contrast, the following Talmudic statement reflects the views that for some Jews, ascetic practices are actually sinful, and that the 613 commanded mitzvot offer sufficient spiritual discipline for anyone seeking to please God.

R. Isaac (reported by R. Dimi) said: "Are not the things prohibited you in the Law enough for you, that you want to prohibit yourself other things." [TALMUD, J. NEDARIM 9:1]

1.2 Quotes from the Tanakh (Hebrew Bible)

Adam and Eve in the Garden

And the Lord God commanded man, saying, "Of every tree of the garden you may freely eat. But of the Tree of Knowledge of good and evil you shall not eat of it, for on the day that you eat thereof, you shall surely die."

[GENESIS 2:16-17 (CJB)]

Moses' Forty Days & Nights on Mount Sinai

The Lord said to Moses: "Inscribe these words for yourself, for according to these words I have formed a covenant with you and with Israel."

He was there with the Lord for forty days and forty nights; he ate no bread and drank no water, and He inscribed upon the tablets the words of the Covenant, the Ten Commandments.

And it came to pass when Moses descended from Mount Sinai, and the two tablets of the testimony were in Moses' hand when he descended from the mountain and Moses did not know that the skin of his face had become radiant while He had spoken with him.

[EXODUS 34:27-29 (CJB)]

When I ascended the mountain to receive the stone tablets, the tablets of the covenant which the Lord made with you, I remained on the mountain forty days and forty nights; I neither ate bread nor drank water;

and the Lord gave me two stone tablets, inscribed by the finger of God, and on them was [inscribed] according to all the words that the Lord spoke with you on the mountain from the midst of the fire on the day of the assembly.

And it came to pass at the end of forty days and forty nights, that the Lord gave me two stone tablets, the tablets of the covenant.

[DEUTERONOMY 9:9-11 (CJB)].

And I fell down before the Lord as before, forty days and forty nights; I neither ate bread nor drank water, because of all your sins you had committed, by doing evil in the eyes of the Lord to anger Him.

[DEUTERONOMY 9:18(CJB)].

The Day of Atonement (Yom Kippur)

And this shall be a statute forever unto you: that in the seventh month, on the tenth day of the month, ye shall afflict your souls, and do no work at all, whether it be one of your own country, or a stranger that sojourneth among you: because on this day atonement will be made for you, to cleanse you. Then, before the LORD, you will be clean from all your sins.

[LEVITICUS 16:29-30 (JPS)].

And ye shall be holy unto Me; for I the LORD am holy, and have set you apart from the peoples, that ye should be Mine.

[LEVITICUS 20:26 (JPS)].

And the LORD spoke unto Moses, saying: Howbeit on the tenth day of this seventh month is the day of atonement; there shall be a holy convocation unto you, and ye shall afflict your souls; and ye shall bring an offering made by fire unto the LORD. And ye shall do no manner of work in that same day; for it is a day of atonement, to make atonement for you before the LORD your God. For whatsoever soul it be that shall not be afflicted in that same day, he shall be cut off from his people. And whatsoever soul it be that doeth any manner of work in that same day, that soul will I destroy from among his people. Ye shall do no manner of work; it is a statute for ever throughout your generations in all your dwellings. It shall be unto you a sabbath of solemn rest, and ye shall afflict your souls; in the ninth day of the month at even, from even unto even, shall ye keep your sabbath.

[Leviticus 23:26-32 (JPS)].

Dietary Restrictions (Kashrut)

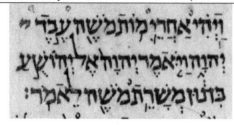

For thou art an holy people unto the LORD thy God, and the LORD hath chosen thee to be a peculiar people unto himself, above all the nations that are upon the earth. For thou art a holy people unto the LORD thy God, and the LORD hath chosen thee to be a peculiar people unto himself, above all the nations that are upon the earth. Thou shalt not eat any abominable thing.

[DEUTERONOMY 14:2-3 (KJV)].

These are the regulations concerning animals, birds, every living thing that moves about in the water and every creature that moves along the ground. You must distinguish between the unclean and the clean, between living creatures that may be eaten and those that may not be eaten.

[LEVITICUS 11:46-47 (NIV)].

The Nazarite Vow

*And the Lord said to Moses, "Say to the people of Israel, When
either a man or a woman makes a special vow, the vow of a
Nazirite to separate himself to the Lord, he shall separate
himself from wine and strong drink; he shall drink no vinegar
made from wine or strong drink, and shall not drink any juice
of grapes or eat grapes, fresh or dried. All the days of his
separation he shall eat nothing that is produced by the
grapevine, not even the seeds or the skins.*

[NUMBERS 6:1-4 (RSV)].

*You are barren and childless, but you are going to become
pregnant and give birth to a son [Samson]. Now see to it that
you drink no wine or other fermented drink and that you do
not eat anything unclean. You will become pregnant and have
a son whose head is never to be touched by a razor because
the boy is to be a Nazirite, dedicated to God from the
womb...Then the woman went to her husband and told him,
"A man of God came to me. He looked like an angel of God,
very awesome. I didn't ask him where he came from, and he
didn't tell me his name. But he said to me, 'You will become
pregnant and have a son. Now then, drink no wine or other
fermented drink and do not eat anything unclean, because*

the boy will be a Nazirite of God from the womb until the day
of his death.'"

[JUDGES 13:3-7 (NIV)].

In her deep anguish Hannah prayed to the Lord, weeping
bitterly. And she made a vow, saying, "Lord Almighty, if you
will only look on your servant's misery and remember me,
and not forget your servant but give her a son [Samuel], then
I will give him to the Lord for all the days of his life, and no
razor will ever be used on his head." [

1 SAMUEL 1:11 (NIV)].

Judges

Wherefore all the children of Israel came to the house of God,
and sat and wept before the Lord: and they fasted that day
till the evening, and offered to him holocausts, and victims of
peace offerings,

[JUDGES 20:26 (DRA)].

Samuel

Sh'mu'el [Samuel] said, "Gather all Isra'el to Mitzpah, and I will pray for you to Adonai." So they gathered together at Mitzpah, drew water and poured it out before Adonai, fasted that day, and said there, "We have sinned against Adonai." Sh'mu'el began serving as judge over the people of Isra'el at Mitzpah.

[[1 SAMUEL 7:5-6 (CJB)]].

They wailed and cried, and they fasted until evening for Sha'ul [Saul], for Y'honatan [Jonathan]his son, for Adonai's [the Lord's] people and for the house of Isra'el; because they had fallen by the sword.

[2 SAMUEL 1:12 (CJB)].

David Fasts for His Son

After Nathan had gone home, the Lord struck the child that Uriah's wife had borne to David, and he became ill. David pleaded with God for the child. He fasted and spent the nights lying in sackcloth b on the ground. The elders of his household stood beside him to get him up from the ground, but he refused, and he would not eat any food with them.

On the seventh day the child died. David's attendants were afraid to tell him that the child was dead, for they thought, "While the child was still living, he wouldn't listen to us when we spoke to him. How can we now tell him the child is dead? He may do something desperate."

David noticed that his attendants were whispering among themselves, and he realized the child was dead. "Is the child dead?" he asked.

"Yes," they replied, "he is dead."

Then David got up from the ground. After he had washed, put on lotions and changed his clothes, he went into the house of the Lord and worshiped. Then he went to his own house, and at his request they served him food, and he ate.

His attendants asked him, "Why are you acting this way? While the child was alive, you fasted and wept, but now that the child is dead, you get up and eat!"

He answered, "While the child was still alive, I fasted and wept. I thought, 'Who knows? The Lord may be gracious to me and let the child live.' But now that he is dead, why should I go on fasting? Can I bring him back again? I will go to him, but he will not return to me."

[2 SAMUEL 12:15-23 (NET)].

Kings

But he [Elijah] himself went a day's journey into the wilderness, and came and sat down under a juniper tree: and he requested for himself that he might die; and said, It is enough; now, O LORD, take away my life; for I am not better than my fathers. And as he lay and slept under a juniper tree, behold, then an angel touched him, and said unto him,

Arise and eat. And he looked, and, behold, there was a cake baken on the coals, and a cruse of water at his head. And he did eat and drink, and laid him down again. And the angel of the LORD came again the second time, and touched him, and said, Arise and eat; because the journey is too great for thee. And he arose, and did eat and drink, and went in the strength of that meat forty days and forty nights unto Horeb the mount of God.

[1 KINGS 19:4-8 (KJV)].

And when Ahab heard those words, he tore his clothes and put sackcloth on his flesh and fasted and lay in sackcloth and went about dejectedly. And the word of the LORD came to Elijah the Tishbite, saying, "Have you seen how Ahab has humbled himself before me? Because he has humbled himself before me, I will not bring the disaster in his days; but in his son's days I will bring the disaster upon his house."

[1 KINGS 21:27-29 (ESV)].

True Fasting Described by Isaiah

Shout out loud! Don't hold back! Raise your voice like a shofar! Proclaim to my people what rebels they are, to the house of Ya'akov [Jacob] their sins. "Oh yes, they seek me day after day and [claim to] delight in knowing my ways. As if they were an upright nation that had not abandoned the rulings of their God, they ask me for just rulings and [claim] to take pleasure in closeness to God, [asking,] 'Why should we fast, if you don't see? Why mortify ourselves, if you don't notice?'

"Here is my answer: when you fast, you go about doing whatever you like, while keeping your laborers hard at work. Your fasts lead to quarreling and fighting, to lashing out with violent blows. On a day like today, fasting like yours will not make your voice heard on high.

"Is this the sort of fast I want, a day when a person mortifies himself? Is the object to hang your head like a reed and spread sackcloth and ashes under yourself? Is this what you call a fast, a day that pleases Adonai?

"Here is the sort of fast I want —releasing those unjustly bound, untying the thongs of the yoke, letting the oppressed go free, breaking every yoke, sharing your food with the hungry, taking the homeless poor into your house, clothing the naked when you see them, fulfilling your duty to your kinsmen!"

Then your light will burst forth like the morning, your new skin will quickly grow over your wound; your righteousness will precede you, and Adonai's glory will follow you. Then you will call, and Adonai will answer; you will cry, and he will say, "Here I am."

[ISAIAH 58:1-9 (CJB)].

Jeremiah

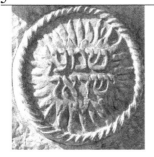

When they fast, I will not hear their cry; and when they offer burnt offering and an oblation, I will not accept them: but I will consume them by the sword, and by the famine, and by the pestilence.

[JEREMIAH 14:12 (KJV)].

Then the word of the Lord came to Jeremiah, saying: "This is what the Lord Almighty, the God of Israel, says: Go and tell the people of Judah and those living in Jerusalem, 'Will you not learn a lesson and obey my words?' declares the Lord. 'Jehonadab son of Rekab ordered his descendants not to drink wine and this command has been kept. To this day they do not drink wine, because they obey their forefather's command. But I have spoken to you again and again, yet you have not obeyed me.

[JEREMIAH 35:12-14 (NIV)].

Therefore go thou, and read in the roll, which thou hast written from my mouth, the words of the LORD in the ears of the people in the LORD's house upon the fasting day: and also thou shalt read them in the ears of all Judah that come out of their cities. It may be they will present their supplication before the LORD, and will return every one from his evil way: for great is the anger and the fury that the LORD hath pronounced against this people ... And it came to pass in the fifth year of Jehoiakim the son of Josiah king of Judah, in the ninth month, that they proclaimed a fast before the LORD to all the people in Jerusalem, and to all the people that came from the cities of Judah unto Jerusalem.

[JEREMIAH 36:6-9 (KJV)].

Joel

Declare a holy fast; call a sacred assembly. Summon the elders and all who live in the land to the house of the LORD your God, and cry out to the LORD.

[JOEL 1:14 (NIV)].

Amos

And I raised up some of your sons for prophets, and some of your young men for Nazirites. Is it not indeed so, O people of Israel?" declares the Lord. "But you made the Nazirites drink wine, and commanded the prophets, saying, 'You shall not prophesy.'"

[AMOS 2:11–12 (ESV)].

Jonah

Jonah began to go into the city, going a day's journey. And he called out, "Yet forty days, and Nineveh shall be overthrown!" And the people of Nineveh believed God. They called for a fast and put on sackcloth, from the greatest of them to the least of them.

[JONAH 3:4-5 (ESV)].

Zechariah

Thus saith the LORD of hosts: The fast of the fourth month, and the fast of the fifth, and the fast of the seventh, and the fast of the tenth, shall be to the house of Judah joy and gladness, and cheerful seasons; therefore love ye truth and peace.

[ZECHARIAH 8:19 (JPS)]

Psalms

Malicious witnesses rise up; they ask me of things that I do not know. They repay me evil for good; my soul is bereft. But I, when they were sick—I wore sackcloth; I afflicted myself with fasting; I prayed with head bowed on my chest. I went about as though I grieved for my friend or my brother; as one who laments his mother, I bowed down in mourning.

[PSALM 35:11-14 (ESV)]

But do thou for me, O God the Lord, for thy name's sake: because thy mercy is good,deliver thou me. For I am poor and needy,and my heart is wounded within me. I am gone like the shadow when it declineth:I am tossed up and down as the locust. My knees are weak through fasting;and my flesh faileth of fatness. I became also a reproach unto them:when they looked upon me they shaked their heads. Help me, O Lord my God:O save me according to thy mercy: that they may know that this is thy hand;that thou, Lord, hast done it.

[PSALM 109:21-27 (KJV)]

Esther

*Then Mordecai bade them to return answer unto Esther:
'Think not with thyself that thou shalt escape in the king's
house, more than all the Jews. For if thou altogether holdest
thy peace at this time, then will relief and deliverance arise to
the Jews from another place, but thou and thy father's house
will perish; and who knoweth whether thou art not come to
royal estate for such a time as this?' Then Esther bade them
return answer unto Mordecai: 'Go, gather together all the
Jews that are present in Shushan, and fast ye for me, and
neither eat nor drink three days, night or day; I also and my
maidens will fast in like manner; and so will I go in unto the
king, which is not according to the law; and if I perish, I
perish.' 17So Mordecai went his way, and did according to all
that Esther had commanded him.*

[ESTHER 4:13-16 (JPS)].

Daniel

---

*In the first year of Darius son of Xerxes a, who was made
ruler over the Babylonian kingdom— in the first year of his
reign, I, Daniel, understood from the Scriptures, according to
the word of the Lord given to Jeremiah the prophet, that the
desolation of Jerusalem would last seventy years.*

*So I turned to the Lord God and pleaded with him in
prayer and petition, in fasting, and in sackcloth and ashes.*

[DANIEL 9:1-3 (NIV)].

*In the third year of Cyrus king of Persia, a word was revealed
to Daniel, who was named Belteshazzar. And the word was
true, and it was a great conflict And he understood the word
and had understanding of the vision. In those days I, Daniel,
was mourning for three weeks. I ate no delicacies, no meat or
wine entered my mouth, nor did I anoint myself at all, for the
full three weeks.*

[DANIEL 10:1-2 (ESV)]

Ezra

Then, there at the Ahava River, I proclaimed a fast; so that we could humble ourselves before our God and ask a safe journey of him for ourselves, our little ones and all our possessions. For I would have been ashamed to ask the king for a detachment of soldiers and horsemen to protect us from enemies along the road, since we had said to the king, "The hand of our God is on all who seek him, for good; but his power and fury is against all who abandon him." So we fasted and asked our God for this, and he answered our prayer.

[EZRA 8:21-23 (CJB)].

Nehemiah

And they said unto me, The remnant that are left of the captivity there in the province are in great affliction and reproach: the wall of Jerusalem also is broken down, and the gates thereof are burned with fire.

And it came to pass, when I heard these words, that I sat down and wept, and mourned certain days, and fasted, and prayed before the God of heaven,

[NEHEMIAH 1:3-4 (KJV)].

On the twenty-fourth day of the same month, the Israelites gathered together, fasting and wearing sackcloth and putting dust on their heads. Those of Israelite descent had separated themselves from all foreigners. They stood in their places and confessed their sins and the sins of their ancestors. They stood where they were and read from the Book of the Law of the Lord their God for a quarter of the day, and spent another quarter in confession and in worshiping the Lord their God.

[NEHEMIAH 9:1-3 (NIV)].

1.3 Other Judaic Texts

Book of Judith

As a widow, Judith stayed inside her home for three years and four months. She had had an upper room built for herself on the roof. She wore sackcloth next to the skin and dressed in widow's weeds. She fasted every day of her widowhood except for the Sabbath eve, the Sabbath itself, the eve of New Moon, the feast of New Moon and the joyful festivals of the House of Israel.

[JUDITH 8:4-6].

Book of Tobit

Prayer is good when accompanied by fasting, almsgiving, and righteousness. A little with righteousness is better than much with wrongdoing. It is better to give alms than to treasure up gold.

[TOBIT 12:8 (RSV)].

Testaments of the Twelve Patriarchs

Ye see therefore, my children, how great things patience worketh, and prayer with fasting. And if ye, therefore, follow after sobriety and purity in patience and humility of heart, the Lord will dwell among you, because He loveth sobriety. And wheresoever the Most High dwelleth, even though a man fall into envy, or slavery, or slander, the Lord who dwelleth in him, for his sobriety's sake not only delivereth him from evil, but also exalteth and glorifieth him . . .

[XI, THE TESTAMENT OF JOSEPH CONCERNING SOBRIETY 10]

The Psalms of Solomon

The righteous continually searcheth his house, To remove utterly (all) iniquity (done) by him in error. He maketh atonement for (sins of) ignorance by fasting and afflicting his soul, And the Lord counteth guiltless every pious man and his house.

[THE PSALMS OF SOLOMON, III:7-8]

Ben Sira

So is it with a man that fasteth for his sins, and goeth again, and doeth the same: who will hear his prayer? or what doth his humbling profit him?

[BEN SIRA 34:26 (KJV W/APOCRYPHA)].

History of the Rechabites

About that time there was in the desert a certain man named Zosimus, who for forty years ate no bread, and drank no wine, and saw not the face of man. This man was entreating God that he might see the way of life of the blessed, and behold an angel of the Lord was sent saying to him, Zosimus, man of God, behold I am sent by the Most High, the God of all, to tell thee that thou shalt journey to the blessed, but shalt not dwell with them. But exalt not thy heart, saying, For forty years I have not eaten bread, for the word of God is more than bread, and the spirit of God is more than wine.

HISTORY OF THE RECHABITES I

The Apocalypse of Abraham

Because you have loved to search me out, and I have named
you 'my friend.' But abstain from every form of food that
comes forth out of the fire, and from the drinking of wine, and
from anointing yourself with oil, for forty days, and then set
forth for me the sacrifice which I have commanded you, in a
place which I will show you on a high mountain, and there I
will show you the ages which have been created and
established by my word, and I will make known to you what
shall come to pass in them on those who have done evil and
righteousness in the generations of men.

[THE APOCALYPSE OF ABRAHAM 9:3].

The Apocalypse of Elijah

Hear, O wise men of the land, concerning the deceivers who will multiply in the last times so that they will set down for themselves doctrines which do not belong to God, setting aside the Law of God, those who have made their belly their God, saying, "The fast does not exist, nor did God create it," making themselves strangers to the covenant of God and robbing themselves of the glorious promises. Now, these are not ever correctly established in the firm faith.

Therefore don't let those people lead you astray. Remember that from the time when He created the heavens, the Lord created the fast for a benefit to men on account of the passions and desires which fight against you so that the evil will not inflame you. "But it is a pure fast which I have created," said the Lord. The one who fasts continually will not sin although jealousy and strife are within him.

Let the pure one fast, but whenever the one who fasts is not pure he has angered the Lord and also the angels. And he has grieved his soul, gathering up wrath for himself for the day of wrath.

[THE APOCALYPSE OF ELIJAH 13-19].

2 Book of the Apocalypse of Baruch

Go therefore and sanctify thyself seven days, and eat no bread, nor drink water, nor speak to anyone. And afterwards come to that place and I will reveal Myself to you, and speak true things with you, and I will give you commandment regarding the method of the times; for they are coming and tarry not.'

And I went there and sat in the valley of Kidron in a cave of the earth, and I sanctified my soul there, and I ate no bread, yet I was not hungry, and I drank no water, yet I thirsted not, and I was there till the seventh day, as He had commanded me.

And afterwards I came to that place where He had spoken with me. And it came to pass at sunset that my soul took much thought, and I began to speak in the presence of the Mighty One . . .

[2 BARUCH 20:5-21:3].

Philo Judaeus of Alexandria (c. 25 BCE. - 45 CE)

*On the tenth day, the fast takes place which they take seriously--
not only those who are zealous about piety and holiness, but
even those who do nothing religious the rest of the time. For all
are astounded, overcome with the sacredness of it; in fact, at
that time, the worse compete with the better in self-control and
virtue. The reputation of the day is due to two reasons: one that
it is a feast and the other that it is purification and escape from
sins for which amnesty has been given by the favors of the
gracious God who has assigned the same honor to repentance
that he has to not committing a single Sin . . .*

PHILO, THE SPECIAL LAWS, I,

*But on this fast it is not lawful to take any food or any drink, in
order that no bodily passion may at all disturb or hinder the
pure operations of the mind; but these passions are wont to be
generated by fullness and satiety, so that at this time men feast,
propitiating the Father of the universe with holy prayers, by
which they are accustomed to solicit pardon for their former
sins, and the acquisition and enjoyment of new blessings.*

[A TREATISE ON THE LIFE OF MOSES, 4:24]

1.4 Additional Judaic Sources

Mishnah and Talmud

When R. Shesheth kept a fast, on concluding his prayer he added the following: Sovereign of the Universe, Thou knowest full well that in the time when the Temple was standing, if a man sinned he used to bring a sacrifice, and though all that was offered of it was its fat and blood, atonement was made for him therewith. Now I have kept a fast and my fat and blood have diminished. May it be Thy will to account my fat and blood which have been diminished as if I had offered them before Thee on the altar, and do Thou favour me.

[BABYLONIAN TALMUD: TRACTATE BERAKOTH, FOLIO 17A].

Our brothers, it is not sackcloth and fasting that cause atonement for our sins. Rather, repentance and good deeds will cause our atonement. This is as we find with regard to the people of Nineveh, that it is not stated about them: And God saw their sackcloth and their fasting. Rather, the verse states: "And God saw their deeds, that they had turned from their evil way" (Jonah 3:10).

TAANIT 16A:

*Should even these seven fast-days have passed without a
favorable answer to the prayers, the people are to avoid and
withdraw from engaging in any joyous occupation, and also to
diminish their business; from the erection of buildings and from
the planting of pleasure-gardens; from betrothals, weddings,
and mutual greetings, like men who are rebuked by the
Omnipotent; (pious) private individuals recommence fasting till
the end of the month of Nissan. If Nissan had passed and then
rain descended, it must be considered a curse, for it is written [I
Samuel, xii. 17]: "Is it not wheat harvest to-day?" . . .*

[TA'ANIT: REGULATING HOW TO FAST FOR RAIN, P. 30].

*Come and hear: For Rabbah b. Samuel taught: One does not
afflict children on the Day of Atonement, but one trains them a
year, or two, before their attaining maturity. That will be right
according to R. Johanan, but according to R. Huna and R.
Nahman, this presents a difficulty. — [These] Rabbis will tell
you: 'Training' here means 'fasting to the end of the day'. But
has 'training' the meaning of 'fasting to the end of the day'? Was
it not taught: What is training? If he was accustomed to eat at
the second hour [eight o'clock], one feeds him now at the third
hour [nine o'clock]; if he was accustomed to eat at the third
hour, one feeds him now at the fourth. Raba b. 'Ulla said, There
are two kinds of training.*

[YOMA: REGULATING FASTING ON THE DAY OF ATONEMENT]

Maimonides (Rambam) (1135- 1204)

A Torah scholar should not be a glutton but should eat only food which will maintain his health. And he should not overeat [even] such foods. He should not run to fill his stomach as those who fill up from food and drink until their stomachs are ready to burst. Regarding such people, it states explicitly in Scripture, "I will scatter dung on your faces, the dung of your holiday offerings" (Malachi 2:3).

[MISHNEH TORAH, DEOT, CH. 5]

We should fast and sound the trumpets in the [following] situations of communal distress: because of the distress that the enemies of the Jews cause the Jews, because of [the passage of] an armed [force], because of a plague, because of a wild animal [on a rampage], because of various species of locusts, because of the black blight and the yellow blight, because of falling buildings, because of an epidemic, because of [the loss of our source of] sustenance, and because of rain [or a lack of it].

[MISHNEH TORAH, SEFER ZEMANIM, TA'ANIYOT, 2:1]

Just as the community should fast because of distress, so too, each individual should fast [when confronted by] distress. What is implied? When an individual to whom a person [feels close] is sick, lost in the desert, or imprisoned, one should fast for his sake, ask for mercy for him in prayer, and say [the passage] Anenu in all the Shemoneh Esreh prayers recited [that day]. One should not fast on the Sabbath, on festivals, on Rosh Chodesh, on Chanukah, or on Purim.

[MISHNEH TORAH, SEFER ZEMANIM, TA'ANIYOT, 1:9]

There are days when the entire Jewish people fast because of the calamities that occurred to them then, to arouse [their] hearts and initiate [them in] the paths of repentance. This will serve as a reminder of our wicked conduct and that of our ancestors, which resembles our present conduct and therefore brought these calamities upon them and upon us. By reminding ourselves of these matters, we will repent and improve [our conduct], as [Leviticus 26:40] states: "And they will confess their sin and the sin of their ancestors."

[MISHNEH TORAH, SEFER ZEMANIM, TA'ANIYOT, 5:1].

These[fasting] days are the following: The Third of Tishrei. *This is the day on which Gedaliah ben Achikam was slain and the ember of Israel that remained was extinguished, causing their exile to become complete.* The Tenth of Tevet. *This is the day Nebuchadnezzar, the wicked, the King of Babylon, camped against Jerusalem and placed the city under siege.* The Seventeenth of Tammuz. *Five tragedies took place on this day: a) The Tablets were broken; b) In the First Temple, the offering of the daily sacrifices was nullified; c) [The walls of] Jerusalem were breached in [the war leading to] the destruction of the Second Temple; d) Apostmos, the wicked, burned a Torah scroll; and e) He erected an idol in the Temple.*

[MISHNEH TORAH, SEFER ZEMANIM, TA'ANIYOT, 5:2].

On the Ninth of Av, *five tragedies occurred: It was decreed that the Jews in the desert would not enter Eretz Yisrael; The First and the Second Temples were destroyed; A large city named Betar was captured. Thousands and myriads of Jews inhabited it. They were ruled by a great king whom the entire Jewish people and the leading Sages considered to be the Messianic king. The city fell to the Romans and they were all slain, causing a national catastrophe equivalent to that of the Temple's destruction. On that day designated for retribution, the wicked Tineius Rufus plowed the site of the Temple and its surroundings, thereby fulfilling the prophecy [Micah 3:12], "Zion will be plowed like a field."*

[MISHNEH TORAH, SEFER ZEMANIM, TA'ANIYOT, 5:3].

And the entire Jewish people follow the custom of fasting at these times and on the Thirteenth of Adar, *in commemoration of the fasts that [the people] took upon themselves in the time of Haman, as mentioned [in Esther 9:31]: "the matter of the fasts and the outcries."*

[MISHNEH TORAH, SEFER ZEMANIM, TA'ANIYOT, 5:5].

Avraham ben ha-Rambam (1186 – 1237CE)

The purpose of the desire for outward retreat is to realize inward retreat, through which one can realize the benefit – the prophetic encounter -- or something similar to it ... The intimate ones – the prophets, their disciples, and the chasidim – would practice retreat in the Temple which contains the burnt offering altar and the incense altar ...

[R. AVRAHAM BEN HARAMBAM, QUOTED IN JEWISH CONTEMPLATIVES].

Zohar

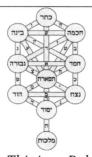

This is as Rabbi Yehuda said, that through his fasting a person weakens his limbs and fire strengthens within him. At that very time, he should [consciously] sacrifice his fat and blood in that fire which is the equivalent of the atoning altar. And Rabbi Elazar when he was sitting in his fast would pray, saying, "It is revealed and known before you G‑d, my G‑d and the G‑d of my forefathers, that I have sacrificed my blood and fat before You and boiled them in the fire of the weakness of my body. May it be Your will that the smell that rises from my mouth at this time be as the fire of the sacrifice on the altar, and be found pleasing before You." So we find that a person actually sacrifices his fat and blood in a fast, and the smell that rises from his mouth is the atoning altar. This is why they [the Sages] have established prayer in the place of sacrifices on the condition that he intends what he says.

QUOTED IN "HEAT YOUR HEART OUT"

How much better it is if a person engages in fasting while studying, for the scent which ascends from the utterances of one who fasts serves as a substitute for actual sacrifice. By means of the "breath" of the words of Torah, uttered in the course of study, the scent of his words ascends on high, unifying and "sweetening" the forces of strict judgment.
For each "breath" of the Torah is a ladder by means of which prayer and the soul ascend above.

SAFED SPIRITUALITY: RULES OF MYSTICAL PIETY, THE BEGINNING OF WISDOM, EDITED BY LAWRENCE FINE, P. 109

Rabbi Schneur Zalman of Liadi (1745 –1812)

Nonetheless, every man of spirit who desires to be close to

G‑d, to repair his soul, to return it to G‑d with the finest and

most preferred repentance, shall be stringent with himself. He

should complete, at least once during his life span, the

number of fasts for every grave sin incurring death at least, if

only death by divine agency.

TANYA CHAPTER 3

Abraham Isaac Kook (1865 – 1935)

The Disadvantage of Fasting: By fasting, we can attain atonement in a way similar to the sacrifice of fats and blood in the Temple service. However, there is an important distinction between fasts and sacrifices. Offering a sacrifice in the holy Temple instilled the powerful message that it should really be the offender's blood spilled and body burned, were it not for God's kindness in accepting a substitute and a ransom. This visceral experience was a humbling encounter, subduing one's negative traits and desires.

Fasting, on the other hand, weakens all forces of the body. Just as chemotherapy treatment poisons other parts of the body as it fights the cancer, so too, fasting saps both our positive and negative energies. Fasting has the unwanted side effect of weakening our energy to help others, perform mitzvot, and study Torah.

Therefore, Rabbi Sheshet added a special prayer when he fasted. He prayed that his fasting would achieve the same atonement as an offering in the Temple, without the undesirable effect of sapping positive energies.

[GOLD FROM THE LAND OF ISRAEL, P. 178]

One whose soul does not wander in the expanses, one who does not seek the light of truth and goodness with all his heart, does not suffer spiritual ruins - but he will also not have his own self-based constructions. Instead, he takes shelter in the shadow of the natural constructions, like rabbits under boulders. But one who has a human soul cannot take shelter in anything other than constructions that he builds with his own spiritual toil.

QUOTED IN ARUTZ SHEVA

Martin Buber (1878 –1965)

*Rabbi Baer of Radoshitz once said to his teacher, the "Seer"
of Lublin: "Show me one general way to the service of God."
The zaddik replied: "It is impossible to tell men what way
they should take. For one way to serve God is through
learning, another through prayer, another through fasting,
and still another through eating. Everyone should carefully
observe what way his heart draws him to, and then choose
this way with all his strength." ...*

*One point in the tale of the "Seer" seems to contradict this,
namely, that among the examples of "ways" we find not only
eating but also fasting. But if we consider this in the general
context of Hasidic teaching, it appears that though
detachment from nature, abstinence from natural life, may,
in the cases of some men, mean the necessary starting-point
of their "way" or, perhaps, a necessary act of self-isolation at
certain crucial moments of existence, it may never mean the
whole way. Some men must begin by fasting, and begin by it
again and again, because it is peculiar to them that only by*

asceticism can they achieve liberation from their
enslavement to the world, deepest heart-searching and
ultimate communion with the Absolute. But never should
asceticism gain mastery over a man's life. A man may only
detach himself from nature in order to revert to it again
and, in hallowed contact with it, find his way to God

[HASIDISM AND MODERN MAN, PP. 68-69]

Gershom Gerhard Scholem (1897 - 1982)

Lurianic kabbalists believed that fasting during these weeks was particularly efficacious in retrieving the "backsliding children," that is, the spirits dwelling in the drops of semen which a man had lost through masturbation or in wet dreams, and which provided "bodies" for demons and evil spirits. The Lurianic identification of the backsliding children (the expression is taken from Jer. 3: 14) and the somewhat punning application of the Hebrew word for "backsliding" (shobabim) clearly caused the choice of this particular period of the year for the penitential exercise. of the year for the penitential exercise. The new tiqqun would restore these "fallen sparks" to the sphere of holiness.

[Sabbatai Sevi: The Mystical Messiah, 1626-1676, translated by R. J. Zwi Werblowsky, p. 293]

Rabbi Pinchas Winston (1959 -)

Food, in fact, is just physical clothing to hide the spiritual sparks within it. It is not apples or vitamins that keep us alive – otherwise, they'd be able to revive dead people as well (which of course, they cannot). It is the sparks they hide inside that feed the soul, which in turn provides life for the body.

This explains how Moses was able to remain on Mount Sinai for 40 consecutive days without eating or drinking. Atop the holy mount, Moses received his life-giving sparks directly from God, without needing to process them through anything physical (i.e. food).

[HOLY SPARKS #3: SOUL FOOD]]

Rabbi Nilton Bonder (1957 -)

When properly followed, fasting represents the perfect merging of our physical and spiritual natures. Fasting means feeding on a nonmaterial food. It is not a passive abstinence from food, but an active feeding on nothing.

[THE KABBALAH OF FOOD , P. 97].

2

CHRISTIAN SOURCES

2.1 Fasting in Christianity

Command to Fast

A direct command to fast is not found in the Gospels. Nevertheless, the words of Jesus clearly assume that his followers would fast. John Wesley made the point that to instruct someone on how and when to do something is equivalent to a command.

> He [Jesus] does not ... expressly enjoin either fasting, giving of alms, or prayer; but his directions how to fast, to give alms, and to pray, are of the same force with such injunctions. For the commanding us to do anything thus, is an unquestionable command to do that thing ... Consequently, the saying, "Give alms, pray, fast" in such a manner, is a clear command to perform all those duties ...
>
> [JOHN WESLEY, SERMON 27, P. 251].

Sons of the Prophets.

Spiritual disciplines are often prompted by impinging secular influences. In Jewish Scripture, prophets at times isolated themselves in groups [2 Kings 4:38; 6:1] seeking to be more receptive to the word of God, or trying to avoid persecution.

On Mount Carmel, prophets Elijah and Elisha, organized what could be called monastic orders. Their followers are known to us as "sons of the prophets."[2 Kings 2:3, 5, 7, 15; 4:1, 38; 5:22].They adopted ascetic spiritual disciplines, often out of necessity, and dictated by the harsh, desolate environment in which the lived.

> *Now the sons of the prophets said to Elisha, "Behold now, the place before you where we are living is too limited for us. Please let us go to the Jordan and each of us take from there a beam, and let us make a place there for ourselves where we may live." So he said, "Go." Then one said, "Please be willing to go with your servants." And he answered, "I shall go."*
>
> [2 KINGS 6:1-3].

The Mount Carmel monastic tradition resurfaced in later religious communities, first Jewish then Christian. Under Roman occupation, many believers countered the paganism of Rome and the compromises Hellenized Jewish authorities by adopting ascetic practices. Jewish sects such as the Essenes and the Therapeutae isolated themselves to countered pagan encroachment

> *The Therapeutae lived separately as anchorites, practiced absolute sexual abstinence, and renounced personal property. They fasted often, prayed daily at set times, and spent hours studying the Old Testament.*
>
> [ON THE CONTEMPLATIVE LIFE, ATTRIBUTED TO PHILO OF ALEXANDRIA].

Desert Fathers

Later, after the Roman persecution of Christians had ended, asceticism became the primary alternative to demonstrating faith and to countering spreading secular influences in the Church. In the 4th century C.E., large numbers of hermits and ascetics began living in the desert of Egypt.

> *When Jesus heard this, he said to him, "One thing you still*
> *lack. Sell all that you have and give the money to the poor,*
> *and you will have treasure in heaven. Then come, follow me."*
>
> [LUKE, 18-22 (NET)].

Many followed the example of Saint Anthony (ca. 251–356) who is recognized as the founder of "desert" monasticism. They renounced the world for a life of solitude, poverty, fasting, charity, and prayer. They engaged in spiritual exercises that became the foundation for the rules that governed later religious orders of both the Eastern Orthodox and Catholic Churches.

> *Around the year 325, Pachomius was inspired by God to*
> *found ... the first monastery in which the monks lived*
> *together under one roof and lived according to a common*
> *Rule... In particular, it emphasizes poverty, fasting, common*
> *prayer, collaboration at work, silence, moderation, and*
> *discretion in eating, and the institution of a general chapter.*
>
> [P. H. GÖRG, THE DESERT FATHERS: ANTHONY AND THE BEGINNINGS OF
> MONASTICISM, P. 83].

2.2 Quotes from the Gospels & Epistles

Jesus Tested in the Wilderness

Then Jesus was led by the Spirit into the wilderness to be tempted by the devil. After fasting forty days and forty nights, he was hungry. The tempter came to him and said, "If you are the Son of God, tell these stones to become bread."

Jesus answered, "It is written: 'Man shall not live on bread alone, but on every word that comes from the mouth of God."

Then the devil took him to the holy city and had him stand on the highest point of the temple. "If you are the Son of God," he said, "throw yourself down. For it is written: 'He will command his angels concerning you, and they will lift you up in their hands, so that you will not strike your foot against a stone.'"

Jesus answered him, "It is also written: 'Do not put the Lord your God to the test.'"

Again, the devil took him to a very high mountain and showed him all the kingdoms of the world and their splendor. "All this I will give you," he said, "if you will bow down and worship me."

Jesus said to him, "Away from me, Satan! For it is written: 'Worship the Lord your God, and serve him only.'"

Then the devil left him, and angels came and attended him.

[MATTHEW 4:1-11 (NIV)]

Jesus Questioned About Fasting

Now John's disciples and the Pharisees were fasting. And people came and said to him, "Why do John's disciples and the disciples of the Pharisees fast, but your disciples do not fast?"

And Jesus said to them, "Can the wedding guests fast while the bridegroom is with them? As long as they have the bridegroom with them, they cannot fast.

The days will come when the bridegroom is taken away from them, and then they will fast in that day.

No one sews a piece of unshrunk cloth on an old garment. If he does, the patch tears away from it, the new from the old, and a worse tear is made.

And no one puts new wine into old wineskins. If he does, the wine will burst the skins—and the wine is destroyed, and so are the skins. But new wine is for fresh wineskins

[MARK 2:18-22 (ESV)].

Jesus Heals a Boy Possessed by an Impure Spirit

And when he came to his disciples, he saw a great multitude about them, and the scribes questioning with them. And straightway all the people, when they beheld him, were greatly amazed, and running to him saluted him. And he asked the scribes, What question ye with them?

And one of the multitude answered and said, Master, I have brought unto thee my son, which hath a dumb spirit; And wheresoever he taketh him, he teareth him: and he foameth, and gnasheth with his teeth, and pineth away: and I spake to thy disciples that they should cast him out; and they could not.

He answereth him, and saith, O faithless generation, how long shall I be with you? how long shall I suffer you? bring him unto me.

And they brought him unto him: and when he saw him, straightway the spirit tare him; and he fell on the ground, and wallowed foaming. And he asked his father, How long is it ago since this came unto him? And he said, Of a child. And ofttimes it hath cast him into the fire, and into the waters, to destroy him: but if thou canst do any thing, have compassion on us, and help us.

Jesus said unto him, If thou canst believe, all things are possible to him that believeth. And straightway the father of the child cried out, and said with tears, Lord, I believe; help thou mine unbelief.

When Jesus saw that the people came running together, he rebuked the foul spirit, saying unto him, Thou dumb and deaf spirit, I charge thee, come out of him, and enter no more into him.

And the spirit cried, and rent him sore, and came out of him: and he was as one dead; insomuch that many said, He is dead.

But Jesus took him by the hand, and lifted him up; and he arose.

And when he was come into the house, his disciples asked him privately, Why could not we cast him out? And he said unto them, This kind can come forth by nothing, but by prayer and fasting.

[MARK 9:14-29 (KJV)]

When You Fast

"When you fast, do not look somber as the hypocrites do, for they disfigure their faces to show others they are fasting. Truly I tell you, they have received their reward in full.

But when you fast, put oil on your head and wash your face, so that it will not be obvious to others that you are fasting, but only to your Father, who is unseen; and your Father, who sees what is done in secret, will reward you.

[MATTHEW 6:16-18 (NIV)].

Paul's Hardships

*Placing no obstacle in anyone's way so our ministry should
not be blemished, in everything, rather, we are commending
ourselves as God's servants: in great endurance, in
tribulations, in hardships, in distresses; in beatings, in
imprisonments, in riots, in labors, in watchings, in fastings; in
purity, in knowledge, in patience, in kindness; in the Holy
Spirit, in genuine love; in the word of truth, in the power of
God; with the weapons of righteousness for the right hand
and for the left; through glory and dishonor, through bad
report and good report; as imposters and yet true; as being
unknown and yet being well-known; as dying and yet, behold,
we live; as being punished and yet not being killed; as being
sorrowful yet always rejoicing; as poor yet enriching many;
as having nothing and yet possessing all things.*

[2 CORINTHIANS 6:3-10 (KJV)]

*For the flesh lusteth against the spirit: and the spirit against
the flesh; for these are contrary one to another: so that you
do not the things that you would.*

[GALATIANS 5:17 (DRV)]

Do not conform to the pattern of this world, but be transformed by the renewing of your mind. Then you will be able to test and approve what God's will is--his good, pleasing and perfect will.

ROMANS 12:2 (NIV)]

Spend your time and energy in training yourself for spiritual fitness. Physical exercise has some value, but spiritual exercise is much more important for it promises a reward in both this life and the next...

[1 TIMOTHY 4:7-9 (NLV)].

But I discipline my body and keep it under control, lest after preaching to others I myself should be disqualified.

[1 CORINTHIANS 9:27(ESV)].

2.3 Early Christian Church

Clement I (88 - 99)

Almsgiving is therefore good even as penitence for sin; fasting is better than prayer, but the giving of alms is better than both; and love "covers a multitude of sins," but prayer from a good conscience rescues from death. Blessed is every man who is found full of these things; for almsgiving lightens sin.

KIRSOPP LAKE, ED. THE APOSTOLIC FATHERS, VOL. 1, LCL 155.

Let them, therefore, with fasting and with prayer make their adjurations, and not with the elegant and well-arranged and fitly-ordered words of learning, but as men who have received the gift of healing from God, confidently, to the glory of God. By your fastings and prayers and perpetual watching, together with your other good works, mortify the works of the flesh by the power of the Holy Spirit

[POPE CLEMENT I, TWO EPISTLES ON VIRGINITY, CH. XII]

Didache (Teaching of the Twelve Apostles)
(c. 70-140)

Before the baptism, moreover, the one who baptizes and the one being baptized must fast, and any others who can. And you must tell the one being baptized to fast for one or two days beforehand. Your fasts must not be identical with those of the hypocrites.

[DIDACHE].

The Shepherd of Hermas (c. 90-140)

This fasting.is very good, provided the commandments of the Lord be observed ... First of all, be on your guard against every evil word, and every evil desire, and purify your heart from all the vanities of this world. If you guard against these things, your fasting will be perfect. And you will do also as follows.

Having fulfilled what is written, in the day on which you fast you will taste nothing but bread and water; and having reckoned up the price of the dishes of that day which you intended to have eaten, you will give it to a widow, or an orphan, or to some person in want, and thus you will exhibit humility of mind, so that he who has received benefit from your humility may fill his own soul, and pray for you to the Lord.

If you observe fasting, as I have commanded you, your sacrifice will be acceptable to God, and this fasting will be written down; and the service thus performed is noble, and sacred, and acceptable to the Lord.

[THE WRITINGS OF THE FATHERS DOWN TO A.D. 325, BK. III, A. ROBERTS & J. DONALDSON].

When you are going to fast, observe it in this way: first, avoid any evil and desire, and purify your heart of all the vain things in the world. Your fast will be perfect if you do this.

[THE SHEPHERD OF HERMAS, FIFTH SIMILITUDE].

Justin Martyr (c.100 – 165)

I will also relate the manner in which we dedicated ourselves to God when we had been made new through Christ; lest, if we omit this, we seem to be unfair in the explanation we are making. As many as are persuaded and believe that what we teach and say is true, and undertake to be able to live accordingly, are instructed to pray and to entreat God with fasting, for the remission of their sins that are past, we praying and fasting with them.

[JUSTIN MARTYR. THE FIRST APOLOGY, CH. LXI

Saint Polycarp of Smyrna (80 – 167)

Wherefore let us forsake the vain doing of the many and their false teachings, and turn unto the word which was delivered unto us from the beginning, being sober unto prayer and constant in fastings, entreating the all-seeing God with supplications that He bring us not into temptation, according as the Lord said, The Spirit is indeed willing, but the flesh is weak.

[POLYCARP 7:2].

Saint Irenaeus (c.130 – c. 202)

For the controversy is not merely as regards the day, but also as regards the form itself of the fast. For some consider themselves bound to fast one day, others two days, others still more, while others [do so during] forty: the diurnal and the nocturnal hours they measure out together as their [fasting] day. And this variety among the observers [of the fasts] had not its origin in our time, but long before in that of our predecessors, some of whom probably, being not very accurate in their observance of it, handed down to posterity the custom as it had, through simplicity or private fancy, been [introduced among them]. And yet nevertheless all these lived in peace one with another, and we also keep peace together. Thus, in fact, the difference [in observing] the fast establishes the harmony of [our common] faith.

[SAINT IRENAEUS OF LYONS, III].

Tertullian (c. 160 – c. 220 AD))

Fasting possesses great power. If practiced with the right intention, it makes one a friend of God.

[ON FASTING].

Let us fast, brethren and sisters, lest tomorrow perchance we die." Openly let us vindicate our disciplines. Sure we are that "they who are in the flesh cannot please God;" not, of course, those who are in the substance of the flesh, but in the care, the affection, the work, the will, of it. Emaciation displeases not us; for it is not by weight that God bestows flesh, any more than He does "the Spirit by measure."

[ON FASTING].

And thus we have already proceeded to examples, in order that, by its profitable efficacy, we may unfold the powers of this duty [fasting] which reconciles God, even when angered, to man.

[ON FASTING].

Origen (c. 184 – c. 253)

Do you still want me to show you what kind of fast it is appropriate for you to practice?

Fast from every sin, take no food of malice, take no feasts of passion, do not burn with any wine of luxury. Fast from evil deeds, abstain from evil words, hold yourself from the worst evil thoughts.

Do not touch the secret loaves of perverse doctrine.

Do not desire the deceptive foods of philosophy which seduce you from truth.

Such a fast pleases God.

[[Homilies on Leviticus, 1-16]]

The Desert Fathers (c. 250-300)

Concerning fasting, do not grieve, as I have said to you before: God does not demand of anyone labors beyond his strength. And indeed, what is fasting if not a punishment of the body in order to humble a healthy body and make it infirm for passions, according to the word of the Apostle: "When I am weak, then am I strong" (II Corinthians 12:10)

, [THE FATHERS OF THE CHURCH, BARSANUPHIUS AND JOHN, P. 103]

An old man was asked, "How can I find God?" He said, "In fasting, in watching, in labours, in devotion, and, above all, in discernment. I tell you, many have injured their bodies without discernment and have gone away from us having achieved nothing. Our mouths smell bad through fasting, we know the Scriptures by heart, we recite all the Psalms of David, but we have not that which God seeks: charity and humility"

[THE WISDOM OF THE DESERT FATHERS, APOPHTHEGMATA PATRUM].

Abba Isidore said, "If you fast regularly, do not be inflated with pride; if you think highly of yourself because of it, then you had better eat meat. It is better for a man to eat meat than to be inflated with pride and glorify himself"
[KELLER, OASIS OF WISDOM: THE WORLDS OF THE DESERT FATHERS & MOTHERS, P. 148]

Abba Hyperechios said, "Fasting is the monk's control over sin. The man who stops fasting is like a stallion who lusts the moment he sees a mare." He also said: "When the monk's body is dried up with fasting, this lifts his soul from the depths. Fasting dries up the channels down which worldly pleasures flow".
BENEDICTA WARD, THE SAYINGS OF THE DESERT FATHERS, P. 27:47-48

Macarius of Egypt (ca. 300 – 391)

This is the mark of Christianity: however much a man toils, and however many righteous deeds he performs, to feel that he has done nothing, and in fasting to say, "This is not fasting," and in praying, "This is not prayer," and in perseverance at prayer, "I have shown no perseverance; I am only just beginning to practice and to take pains"; and even if he is righteous before God, he should say, "I am not righteous, not I; I do not take pains, but only make a beginning every day."

[AQUILINA, THE WAY OF THE FATHERS: PRAYING WITH THE EARLY CHRISTIANS, #574]

A present was made of a newly gathered bunch of grapes to St. Macarius: the holy man carried it to a neighbouring monk who was sick; he sent it to another: it passed in like manner to all the cells in the desert, and was brought back to Macarius, who was exceedingly rejoiced to perceive the. the abstinence of his brethren, but would not eat of the grapes himself.

[ADAPTED FROM THE LIVES OF THE FATHERS, MARTYRS, AND OTHER PRINCIPAL SAINTS, VOL.1, BY ALBAN BUTLER, P. 25]

Saint Basil the Great (330–379)

*Do you think that I am resting the origin of fasting on the Law?
Why, fasting is even older than the Law. If you wait a little, you
will discover the truth of what I have said. Do not suppose that
fasting originated with the Day of Atonement, appointed for
Israel on the tenth day of the seventh month. No, go back
through history and inquire into the ancient origins of fasting. It
is not a recent invention; it is an heirloom handed down by our
fathers. Everything distinguished by antiquity is venerable. Have
respect for the antiquity of fasting. It is as old as humanity itself;
it was prescribed in Paradise.*

[HOMILY ON FASTING, 3].

*Fasting gives birth to prophets and strengthens the powerful;
fasting makes lawgivers wise. Fasting is a good safeguard for
the soul, a steadfast companion for the body, a weapon for the
valiant, and a gymnasium for athletes. Fasting repels
temptations, anoints unto piety; it is the comrade of
watchfulness and the artificer of chastity. In war it fights
bravely, in peace it teaches stillness. It sanctifies the Nazirite21
and perfects the Priest. For it is not possible to dare to perform
sacred actions without fasting, not only in the mystical and true*

*worship of the present era, but also in the symbolic worship
offered according to the Law.*

[HOMILY ON FASTING, 20].

*Do not, however, define the benefit that comes from fasting
solely in terms of abstinence from foods. For true fasting consists
in estrangement from vices. "Loose every burden of iniquity."
Forgive your neighbor the distress he causes you; forgive him his
debts. "Fast not for quarrels and strifes." You do not eat meat,
but you devour your brother. You abstain from wine, but do not
restrain yourself from insulting others. You wait until evening to
eat, but waste your day in law courts. Let us fast an acceptable
and very pleasing fast to the Lord. True fast is the estrangement
from evil, temperance of tongue, abstinence from anger,
separation from desires, slander, falsehood and perjury.
Privation of these is true fasting.*

[HOMILY ON FASTING, 10].

*Will you not conceive a desire for the table in the Kingdom of
Heaven, for which fasting here on earth is assuredly a
preparation? Do you not know that by immoderate satiety you
fatten for yourself the worm that torments? For who amid lavish
feasting and perpetual delectation has become the partaker of
any spiritual gift?*

[HOMILY ON FASTING, 50].

Saint Ambrose (c. 340-397)

If what the Apostle has said is not enough, let them hear the Prophet saying, I chastened myself with fasting. He therefore who fasts not is uncovered and naked and exposed to wounds. And if Adam had clothed himself with fasting he would not have been found to be naked. Nineveh delivered itself from death by fasting. And the Lord Himself says, This kind goeth not out but by prayer and fasting.

[ST. AMBROSE, LETTERS #42.11].

That is why the lord Jesus, wishing to fortify us against the temptations of the Devil, fasted when he was himself about to struggle with him, so that we should know that without fasting we would be unable to overcome the allurements of evil.

AMBROSE OF MILAN: POLITICAL LETTERS AND SPEECHES, P. 301

Saint Jerome (c. 347–420)

Be on your guard when you begin to mortify your body by abstinence and fasting, lest you imagine yourself to be perfect and a saint; for perfection does not consist in this virtue. It [fasting] is only a help; a disposition; a means though a fitting one, for the attainment of true perfection

[LIPPMANN, A PREFACE TO MORALS, P. 161].

Again, God by the mouth of Isaiah says what fast He did not choose: "In the day of your fast ye find pleasure, and afflict the lowly: ye fast for strife and debate, and to smite with the fist of wickedness. It is not such a fast that I have chosen, saith the Lord." What kind He has chosen He thus teaches: "Deal thy bread to the hungry, and bring the houseless poor into thy house. When thou seest the naked cover him, and hide not thyself from thine own flesh." He did not therefore reject fasting, but showed what He would have it to be... If God does not desire fasting, how is it that in Leviticus He commands the whole people in the seventh month, on the tenth day of the month, to fast until the evening, and threatens that he who does not afflict his soul shall die and be cut off from his people?

[SCHAFF, NICENE & POST-NICENE FATHERS OF THE CHRISTIAN CHURCH, P. 402]

Saint John Chrysostom (c. 349–407)

For let not the mouth only fast, but also the eye, and ear, and the feet, and the hands, and all the members of our bodies. Let the hands fast, by being pure from rapine and avarice. Let the feet fast, but ceasing from running to the unlawful spectacles. Let the eyes fast, being taught never to fix themselves rudely upon handsome countenances, or to busy themselves with strange beauties. For looking is the food of the eyes, but if this be such as is unlawful or forbidden, it mars the fast; and upsets the whole safety of the soul; but if it be lawful and safe, it adorns fasting.

For it would be among things the most absurd to abstain from lawful food because of the fast, but with the eyes to touch even what is forbidden. Dost thou not eat flesh? Feed not upon lasciviousness by means of the eyes. Let the ear fast also. The fasting of the ear consists in refusing to receive evil speakings and calumnies. "Thou shalt not receive a false report," it says.

[ON THE PRIESTHOOD; ASCETIC TREATISES; HOMILY III, 8,11]

The honour of fasting consists not in abstinence from food, but in withdrawing from sinful practices; since he who limits his fasting only to an abstinence from meats, is one who especially disparages it. Dost thou fast? Give me proof of it by thy works!

[HOMILY III].

Sharpen thy sickle, which thou hast blunted through gluttony— sharpen it by fasting. Lay hold of the pathway which leads towards heaven; rugged and narrow as it is, lay hold of it, and journey on. And how mayest thou be able to do these things? By subduing thy body, and bringing it into subjection. For when the way grows narrow, the corpulence that comes of gluttony is a great hindrance. Keep down the waves of inordinate desires. Repel the tempest of evil thoughts. Preserve the bark; display much skill, and thou hast become a pilot. But we shall have the fast for a groundwork and instructor in all these things.

[ON THE PRIESTHOOD; ASCETIC TREATISES].

Do you fast? Prove it by doing good works. If you see someone in need, take pity on them. If you see a friend being honored, don't get jealous of him. For a true fast, you cannot fast only with your mouth. You must fast with your eye, your ear, your feet, your hands, and all parts of your body.

[ON FASTING].

As bodily food fattens the body, so fasting strengthens the soul. Imparting it an easy flight, it makes it able to ascend on high, to contemplate lofty things, and to put the heavenly higher than the pleasant and pleasurable things of life.

[ST. JOHN CHRYSOSTOM].

Saint Augustine (354–430)

Fasting punishes you, but brings no refreshment to anyone else. Your restriction will be fruitful if it brings amplitude to another. So you have deprived yourself, have you? But to whom do you mean to give what you have denied yourself? How do you intend to dispose of what you went without? How many poor people might grow fat on that luncheon we missed! ... If you give your bread grudgingly, you have lost both food and merit....How swiftly are the prayers of those who do good works accepted! ... Do you want your prayer to fly to God? Then make two wings for it, fasting and almsgiving.

<u>EXPOSITIONS OF THE PSALMS, PP. 263-4</u>

Fasting cleanses the soul, raises the mind, subjects one's flesh to the spirit, renders the heart contrite and humble, scatters the clouds of concupiscence, quenches the fire of lust, and kindles the true light of chastity. Enter again into yourself.

[<u>"ON PRAYER AND FASTING", QUOTED BY ST. THOMAS AQUINAS</u>].

Fasting must not seem to you of little importance or superfluous. Those who fast, in accordance with the Church's customs, should not think to themselves: What is the point of fasting? You shorten your life, you bring about something negative. Can God want you to torment yourself? It would be cruel if he took pleasure in your suffering ... But you should respond to the tempter in this way: I will certainly impose privation, but it is so that he will forgive me, to be pleasing in his eyes, that I may enjoy his delightfulness..."

[SERMON 400 DE UTILITATE IEIUNI].

But now the necessity of habit is sweet to me, and against this sweetness must I fight, lest I be enthralled by it. Thus I carry on a daily war by fasting, constantly bringing my body into subjection...

[THE CONFESSIONS, CH. XXXI].

It is not by change of place that we can come nearer to Him who is in every place, but by the cultivation of pure desires and virtuous habits.

[ON CHRISTIAN DOCTRINE, P. 8].

Saint John Cassian (c. 360–435)

In the same way, fasting, vigils, scriptural meditation, nakedness and total deprivation do not constitute perfection but are the means to perfection. They are not in themselves the endpoint of a discipline, but an end is attained to through them

[CONFERENCES, P. 42].

And therefore a man will never be able to gain perfect purity, if he hopes to secure it by means of abstinence alone, i.e., bodily fasting, unless he knows that he ought to practise it for this reason that when the flesh is brought low by means of fasting, he may with greater ease enter the lists against other faults, as the flesh has not been habituated to gluttony and surfeiting.

[CONFERENCES, CH. XXVI].

In order to preserve the mind and body in a perfect condition, abstinence from food is not alone sufficient: unless the other virtues of the mind as well are joined to it ... And so humility must first be learned ... anger should be controlled ... vainglory should be despised, the disdainfulness of pride trampled underfoot, and the shifting and wandering thoughts of the mind restrained by continual recollection of God.

[THE TRAINING OF A MONK & THE EIGHT DEADLY SINS, ABSTINENCE] CHAPTER X]

Hesychios the Priest (c. 400–475?)

Humility, fasting, prayer, watchfulness. These are the tools which advance men and women toward holiness, and they are the fruits, too, of that advancement. Humility brings us to a more realistic and understanding view of ourselves, and thus of the grace of God.

Fasting trains the body, so long left to unrestrained gluttony, and through its training brings clarity to the mind and soul. Prayer lifts our whole being into the embrace of God and propels us to divine union.

Finally, watchfulness brings our whole mind and soul to rest in the heart, there to know the love and grace of God. It is the tool by which we are guided by Christ to know good from evil, to maintain the former in our person and repel the latter before it has the opportunity to work harm in our lives.

The combined use of these tools brings us closer to Christ, who has promised that whoever knocks, to him the door shall be opened.

[HESYCHIOS THE PRIEST].

Pope Leo the Great (c. 400–461)

But there are three things which most belong to religious actions, namely prayer, fasting, and almsgiving, in the exercising of which while every time is accepted, yet that ought to be more zealously observed, which we have received as hallowed by tradition from the apostles: even as this tenth month brings round again to us the opportunity when according to the ancient practice we may give more diligent heed to those three things of which I have spoken.

For by prayer we seek to propitiate God, by fasting we extinguish the lusts of the flesh, by alms we redeem our sins: and at the same time God's image is throughout renewed in us, if we are always ready to praise Him, unfailingly intent on our purification and unceasingly active in cherishing our neighbour. This threefold round of duty, dearly beloved, brings all other virtues into action: it attains to God's image and likeness and unites us inseparably with the Holy Spirit. Because in prayer faith remains steadfast, in fastings life remains innocent, in almsgiving the mind remains kind.

[SERMON 12].

The right practice of abstinence is needful not only to the mortification of the flesh but also to the purification of the mind. For the mind then only keeps holy and spiritual fast when it rejects the food of error and the poison of falsehood.

[SERMON 46].

As then we must with the whole heart obey the Divine commands and sound doctrine, so we must use all foresight in abstaining from wicked imaginations. For the mind then only keeps holy and spiritual fast when it rejects the food of error and the poison of falsehood, which our crafty and wily foe plies us with more treacherously now, when by the very return of the venerable Festival, the whole church generally is admonished to understand the mysteries of its salvation.

[SERMON 46].

Saint John Climacus (c. 525-606)

Attend and you will hear Him who says: "Spacious and broad is the way of gluttony that leads to the perdition of fornication, and many there are who go in by it; because narrow is the gate and hard is the way of fasting that leads to the life of purity, and few there are who go in by it [Matthew vii, 13—14]."

[THE LADDER OF DIVINE ASCENT, STEP 14.29].

Fasting is the coercion of nature and the cutting out of everything that delights the palate, the prevention of lust, the uprooting of bad thoughts, deliverance from dreams, purity of prayer, the light of the soul, the guarding of the mind, deliverance from blindness, the door of compunction, humble sighing, glad contrition, a lull in chatter, a means to silence, a guard of obedience, lightening of sleep, health of body, agent of dispassion, remission of sins, the gate of Paradise and its delight.

[THE LADDER OF DIVINE ASCENT, STEP 14.33].

2.4 Popes, Saints and Theologians

Saint Peter Chrysologus (c. 380 – c. 450)

Prayer, mercy and fasting: These three are one, and they give life to each other. Fasting is the soul of prayer; mercy is the lifeblood of fasting. Let no one try to separate them; they cannot be separated. If you have only one of them or not all together, you have nothing.

So if you pray, fast; if fast, show mercy; if you want your petition to be heard, hear the petition of others. When you fast, see the fasting of others. If you hope for mercy, show mercy. If you look for kindness, show kindness. If you want to receive, give.

[PRAYER, FASTING AND MERCY].

Saint Benedict (c. 480 – 547)

O Lord, I place myself in your hands and dedicate myself to you. I pledge myself to do your will in all things: To love the Lord God with all my heart, all my soul, all my strength. Not to kill. Not to steal. Not to covet. Not to bear false witness. To honor all persons. Not to do to another what I would not wish done to myself. To chastise the body. Not to seek after pleasures. To love fasting.

[SAINT BENEDICT, RULE, IV].

Pope Gregory I (c.540 – 604)

Every day you provide your bodies with food to keep them from failing. In the same way, your good works should be the daily nourishment of your hearts. Your bodies are fed with food and your spirits with good works. You should deny not your soul, which is going to live forever, what you grant to your body, which is going to die.

[BE FRIENDS OF GOD, P. 86

The one who does not give to the poor what he has saved but keeps it for later to satisfy his own appetite, does not fast for God.

[QUOTED IN "GIVE YOUR FASTING TWO WINGS"].

That lust follows the addiction to gluttony is testified by the prophet, who denounces hidden things, while he speaks openly, saying: "The chief of the cooks destroyed the walls of Jerusalem. For the "chief of the cooks" is the stomach, because cooks take great care so that they can fill the stomach with pleasant food. But the "walls of Jerusalem" are the virtues of the soul, elevated to a desire for supernal peace. Therefore, the chief of the cooks "destroys the walls of Jerusalem," because when the belly is held in gluttony, the virtues of the soul are destroyed through lust.

[THE BOOK OF PASTORAL RULE, P. 137]

Saint Hildegard of Bingen (1098 – 1179)

Also, temper all your works with moderation, that is to say, all your abstinence, your fasting, your vigils, and your prayers, for temperance sustains your body and soul with the proper measure, lest they fail. It reminds an honorable person that he is ashes and shall return to ashes [cf. Gen 3.19], and that he can hold his office only so long as God wishes. Temperance finds no joy in the company of sinners, nor does it join in the pomp and vanity of this world; rather, it reminds people of the bitterness of punishment and perdition.

[THE LETTERS OF HILDEGARD OF BINGEN, VOL. III]

Saint Francis of Assisi (1181– 1226)

And let them fast from the Feast of All Saints until Christmas. Indeed may those who voluntarily fast the holy lent, which begins at Epiphany and for the forty days that follow, which the Lord consecrated with His own holy fast, be blessed by the Lord, and let those who do not wish to do so not be constrained. But let them fast the other lent until the day of the Resurrection of the Lord. At other times however they are not bound to fast, except on Fridays. Indeed in time of manifest necessity the friars are not bound to the corporal fast.

[THE RULE OF ST FRANCIS, CHAPTER III]

Saint Thomas Aquinas (1225 – 1274)

For he who fasts, is light and active, and prays wakefully, and quenches his evil lusts, makes God propitious, and humbles his proud stomach. And he who prays with his fasting, has two wings, lighter than the winds themselves.

[CATENA AUREA (GOLDEN CHAIN): ST. MATTHEW].

An act is virtuous through being directed by reason to some virtuous good. Now this is consistent with fasting, because fasting is practiced for a threefold purpose. First, in order to bridle the lusts of the flesh, wherefore the Apostle says (2 Cor. 6:5,6): "In fasting, in chastity," since fasting is the guardian of chastity. For, according to "Venus is cold when Ceres and Bacchus are not there," that is to say, lust is cooled by abstinence in meat and drink.

Secondly, we have recourse to fasting in order that the mind may arise more freely to the contemplation of heavenly things: hence it is related (Dan. 10) of Daniel that he received a revelation from God after fasting for three weeks.

*Thirdly, in order to satisfy for sins: wherefore it is written (Joel 2:12): "Be converted to Me with all your heart, in fasting and in weeping and in mourning." The same is declared by Augustine in a sermon [*Serm. lxxii (ccxxx, de Tempore)]: "Fasting cleanses the* *soul, raises the mind, subjects one's flesh to the spirit, renders the heart contrite and humble, scatters the clouds of concupiscence, quenches the fire of lust, kindles the true light of chastity."*

[Summa Theologica Question 147: OF FASTING].

Now it has been stated above that fasting is useful as atoning for and preventing sin, and as raising the mind to spiritual things. And everyone is bound by the natural dictate of reason to practice fasting as far as it is necessary for these purposes. Wherefore fasting in general is a matter of precept of the natural law, while the fixing of the time and manner of fasting as becoming and profitable to the Christian people, is a matter of precept of positive law established by ecclesiastical authority: the latter is the Church fast, the former is the fast prescribed by nature.

Fasting considered in itself denotes something not eligible but penal: yet it becomes eligible in so far as it is useful to some end. Wherefore considered absolutely it is not binding under precept, but it is binding under precept to each one that stands in need of such a remedy. And since men, for the most part, need this remedy, both because "in many things we all offend" (James 3:2), and because "the flesh lusteth against the spirit" (Gal. 5:17), it was fitting that the Church should appoint certain fasts to be kept by all in common

[Summa Theologica Question 147: OF FASTING Article. 3].

Meister Eckhart (1260 – 1327)

All pious practices—praying, reading, singing, watching, fasting, penance, or whatever discipline it be—were contrived to catch and keep us from things alien and ungodly.

MEISTER ECKHART - VOLUME 2, P. 19

... free thy self from all that is contingent, entangling, and cumbersome and direct thy mind always to gazing upon God in thy heart with a steadfast look that never wavers: as for other spiritual exercises— fasting, watching and prayer— direct them all to this one end, and practise them so far as they may be helpful thereto, so wilt thou win to perfection.

MEISTER ECKHART'S SERMONS, P. 51

Saint Catherine of Siena (1347 – 1380)

Now the soul who wishes to rise above imperfection should await My Providence in the House of Self-Knowledge, with the light of faith, as did the disciples, who remained in the house in perseverance and in watching, and in humble and continual prayer, awaiting the coming of the Holy Spirit. She should remain fasting and watching, the eye of her intellect fastened on the doctrine of My Truth, and she will become humble because she will know herself in humble and continual prayer and holy and true desire.

[DIALOGUE OF ST. CATHERINE OF SIENA]

Saint Thomas More (1478 – 1535)

The scripture is full of places that prove fasting to be not the invention of man but the institution of God, and to have many more profits than one. And that the fasting of one man may do good unto another, our Saviour showeth himself where he saith that some kind of devils cannot be cast out of one man by another "without prayer and fasting." And therefore I marvel that they take this way against fasting and other bodily penance.

DIALOGUE OF COMFORT AGAINST TRIBULATION

Saint Ignatius of Loyola (1491 – 1556)

As to foods, one ought to have the greatest and most entire abstinence, because as the appetite is more ready to act inordinately, so temptation is more ready in making trial, on this head. And so abstinence in foods, to avoid disorder, can be kept in two ways, one by accustoming oneself to eat coarse foods; the other, if one takes delicate foods, by taking them in small quantity.

[THE SPIRITUAL EXERCISES OF ST. IGNATIUS OF LOYOLA, AS TO EATING]

Saint Teresa of Ávila (1515 – 1582)

Our primitive rule states that we must pray without ceasing. If we do this with all the care possible -- for unceasing prayer is the most important aspect of the rule -- the fasts, the disciplines, and the silence the order commands will not be wanting. For you already know that if prayer is to be genuine, it must be helped by these other things; prayer and comfortable living are incompatible.

[THE WAY OF PERFECTION].

Saint Francis de Sales (1567 – 1622)

To treat of fasting and of what is required to fast well, we must, at the start, understand that of itself fasting is not a virtue. The good and the bad, as well as Christians and pagans, observe it. The ancient philosophers observed it and recommended it. They were not virtuous for that reason, nor did they practice virtue in fasting. Oh, no, fasting is a virtue only when it is accompanied by conditions which render it pleasing to God. Thus it happens that it profits some and not others, because it is not undertaken by all in the same manner.

[THE SERMONS OF ST. FRANCIS DE SALES: FOR LENT

If you are able to fast, you will do well to observe some days beyond what are ordered by the Church, for besides the ordinary effect of fasting in raising the mind, subduing the flesh, confirming goodness, and obtaining a heavenly reward, it is also a great matter to be able to control greediness, and to keep the sensual appetites and the whole body subject to the law of the Spirit; and although we may be able to do but little, the enemy nevertheless stands more in awe of those whom he knows can fast.

[INTRODUCTION TO THE DEVOUT LIFE. CH. 23].

Fasting and labor both exhaust and subdue the body. If your work is necessary or profitable to God's Glory, I would rather see you bear the exhaustion of work than of fasting. Such is the mind of the Church, who dispenses those who are called to work for God or their neighbor even from her prescribed fasts. One man finds it hard to fast, another finds it as hard to attend the sick, to visit prisons, to hear confessions, preach, minister to the afflicted, pray, and the like. And the last hardship is better than the other; for while it subdues the flesh equally, it brings forth better fruit.

[INTRODUCTION TO THE DEVOUT LIFE. CH. 23].

Pope Clement XIII (1693 – 1769).

After all, it is always necessary to subdue concupiscence, for it is written, "Do not follow behind your desires, and do not turn away from your will." Let the faithful easily turn their attention during this most holy time of year to lessening the intemperance of the body by fasting.

[APPETENTE SACRO (ON THE SPIRITUAL ADVANTAGES OF FASTING)].

Rather, penance also demands that we satisfy divine justice with fasting, almsgiving, prayer, and other works of the spiritual life. Every wrongdoing--be it large or small--is fittingly punished, either by the penitent or by a vengeful God.

[APPETENTE SACRO (ON THE SPIRITUAL ADVANTAGES OF FASTING)].

Saint Alphonsus De Ligouri (1696 – 1787)

He that gratifies the taste will readily indulge the other senses; for, having lost the spirit of recollection, he will easily commit faults, by indecent words and by unbecoming gestures. But the greatest evil of intemperance is that it exposes chastity to great danger. 'Repletion of the stomach,' says St. Jerome, 'is the hotbed of lust.' Saint Basil: "Penance without fasting is useless and vain; by fasting [we] satisfy God."

[SAINT ALPHONSUS DE LIGOURI].

Therese of Lisieux (1873 – 1897)

Last year, during Lent, I felt stronger than ever, and I noticed that I lost none of my energy until Easter, in spite of keeping the full fast. But in the early hours of Good Friday, Jesus gave me cause to hope that I would be joining Him in Heaven before long. The very memory of that moment is delightful!

[THE STORY OF A SOUL: THE AUTOBIOGRAPHY OF THE LITTLE FLOWER]

Pope Pius XII (1876 – 1958)

From the very earliest time, the custom was observed of administering the Eucharist to the faithful who were fasting. Towards the end of the fourth century fasting was prescribed by many Councils for those who were going to celebrate the Eucharistic Sacrifice. So it was that the Council of Hippo in the year 393 issued this decree: "The Sacrament of the altar shall be offered only by those who are fasting." Shortly afterwards, in the year 397, the Third Council of Carthage issued this same command, using the very same words. At the beginning of the fifth century this custom can be called quite common and immemorial. Hence St. Augustine affirms that the Holy Eucharist is always received by people who are fasting and likewise that this custom is observed throughout the entire world.

[CONCERNING THE DISCIPLINE TO BE OBSERVED WITH RESPECT TO THE EUCHARISTIC FAST].

St Padre Pio (1887 –1968)

God enriches the soul which empties itself of everything.
The life of a Christian is nothing but a perpetual struggle
against self; there is no flowering of the soul to the beauty of
its perfection except at the price of pain.

[PADRE PIO: THE STIGMATIST]

Pope Paul VI (1897 – 1978)

This exercise of bodily mortification—far removed from any form of stoicism—does not imply a condemnation of the flesh which sons of God deign to assume. On the contrary, mortification aims at the "liberation" of man, who often finds himself, because of concupiscence, almost chained by his own senses. Through "corporal fasting" man regains strength and the "wound inflicted on the dignity of our nature by intemperance is cured by the medicine of a salutary abstinence."

[Paenitemini (Apostolic Constitution On Penance) 1966].

Saint Maria Faustina Kowalska (1905–1938)

Our meals shall be such that not even the poor will have any reason to envy us... Fasts, especially the two great ones, will be observed strictly, according to the original spirit. The food should be the same for all the nuns without exception so that communal life may be kept pure. This refers not only to food but to clothing and the furnishing of cells as well.

[DIARY OF SAINT MARIA FAUSTINA KOWALSKA, #546].

Interior mortifications take the first place, but besides this, we must practice exterior mortifications, strictly determined, so that all can practice them. These are: on three days a week, Wednesday, Friday and Saturday, there will be a strict fast; each Friday, all the sisters – each one in her own cell – will take the discipline for the length of the recitation of Psalm 50, and all will do this at the same time; namely, three o'clock; and this will be offered for dying sinners. During the two great fasts, ember days and vigils, the food will consist of a piece of bread and some water, once a day.

[DIARY OF SAINT MARIA FAUSTINA KOWALSKA, #565].

Mother Teresa (1910 – 1997)

We too are called to withdraw at certain intervals into deeper silence and aloneness with God, together as a community as well as personally; to be alone with Him – not with our books, thoughts, and memories but completely stripped of everything – to dwell lovingly in His presence, silent, empty, expectant, and motionless. We cannot find God in noise or agitation.

[IN THE HEART OF THE WORLD: THOUGHTS, STORIES AND PRAYERS, P. 10].

Yes, you must live life beautifully and not allow the spirit of the world that makes gods out of power, riches, and pleasure make you forget that you have been created for greater things – to love and to be loved.

MOTHER TERESA, HERE OWN WORDS

Pope John Paul II (1920 – 2005)

Fasting is to reaffirm to oneself what Jesus answered Satan when he tempted him at the end of his 40 days of fasting in the wilderness: "Man shall not live by bread alone but by every word that proceeds from the mouth of God" (Mt 4:4)...

Today, especially in affluent societies, it is difficult to grasp the meaning of these Gospel words. Consumerism, instead of satisfying needs, constantly creates new ones, often generating excessive activism. Everything seems necessary and urgent and one risks not even finding the time to be alone with oneself for a while . . . Penitential fasting is obviously something very different from a therapeutic diet, but in its own way, it can be considered therapy for the soul. In fact practiced as a sign of conversion, it helps one in the interior effort of listening to God.

[Penitential Fasting Is Therapy for the Soul].

Today, especially in affluent societies, St. Augustine's warning is more timely than ever: 'Enter again into yourself.' Yes, we must enter again into ourselves, if we want to find ourselves. Not only our spiritual life is at stake, but indeed, our personal, family and social equilibrium, itself.

[PENITENTIAL FASTING IS THERAPY FOR THE SOUL].

One of the meanings of penitential fasting is to help us recover an interior life. The effort of moderation in food also extends to other things that are not necessary, and this is a great help to the spiritual life. Moderation, recollection and prayer go hand in hand. . . . This principle can be appropriately applied to the mass media. Their usefulness is indisputable, but they must not become the "masters" of our life. In how many families does television seem to replace personal conversation rather than to facilitate it! A certain "fasting" also in this area can be healthy, both for devoting more time to reflection and prayer, and for fostering human relations.

PENITENTIAL FASTING IS THERAPY FOR THE SOU]

Pope Benedict XVI (1927 –)

Fasting means abstaining from food, but includes other forms of self-denial to promote a more sober lifestyle. But that still isn't the full meaning of fasting, which is the external sign of the internal reality of our commitment to abstain from evil with the help of God and to live the Gospel . . .

[GENERAL AUDIENCE]

In our own day, fasting seems to have lost something of its spiritual meaning, and has taken on, in a culture characterized by the search for material well-being, a therapeutic value for the care of one's body. Fasting certainly brings benefits to physical well-being, but for believers, it is, in the first place, a "therapy" to heal all that prevents them from conformity to the will of God.

[MESSAGE FOR LENT 2009].

Through fasting and praying, we allow Him to come and satisfy the deepest hunger that we experience in the depths of our being: the hunger and thirst for God.

[MESSAGE FOR LENT 2009].

It seems abundantly clear that fasting represents an important ascetical practice, a spiritual arm to do battle against every possible disordered attachment to ourselves. Freely chosen detachment from the pleasure of food and other material goods helps the disciple of Christ to control the appetites of nature, weakened by original sin, whose negative effects impact the entire human person. Quite opportunely, an ancient hymn of the Lenten Liturgy exhorts: 'Let us use sparingly words, food and drink, sleep and amusements. May we be more alert in the custody of our senses.' Since all of us are weighed down by sin and its consequences, fasting is proposed to us as an instrument to restore friendship with God.

[MESSAGE FOR LENT 2009].

True fasting, as the divine Master repeats elsewhere, is rather to do the will of the Heavenly Father, who "sees in secret, and will reward you" (Mt 6,18). He Himself sets the example, answering Satan, at the end of the forty days spent in the desert that "man shall not live by bread alone, but by every word that proceeds from the mouth of God" (Mt 4,4). The true fast is thus directed to eating the "true food," which is to do the Father's will (cf. Jn 4,34).

[MESSAGE FOR LENT 2009].

Pope Francis (1936 -).

Fasting is also a caress: Christianity is not a heartless set of rules, a list of formal observances for people who put on the good face of hypocrisy to hide a heart empty of charity. Christianity is the very "flesh" of Christ, who bends down without shame to those who suffer. What helps to explain this contrast to us is the dialogue in the Gospel between Jesus and the disciples of John, who are criticizing those who don't respect fasting. The fact is that the scholars of the law had turned the observance of the commandments into a "formality," turning "religious life" into "an ethics" and forgetting its roots, which is "a story of salvation, of election, of covenant. "

[ENCOUNTERING TRUTH: MEETING GOD IN THE EVERYDAY, 183]

Fasting makes sense if it really affects our security, and also if a benefit to others comes from it, if it helps us to grow in the spirit of the Good Samaritan, who bends down to his brother in need and takes care of him. Fasting involves choosing a sober life, which does not waste, which does not "discard". Fasting helps us to train the heart to essentiality and sharing.

It is a sign of awareness and responsibility in the face of injustices, abuses, especially towards the poor and the little ones, and is a sign of our trust in God and His providence.

[ASH WEDNESDAY HOMILY 2014].

Nutritional disorders can only be combatted by the cultivation of lifestyles inspired by gratitude for the gifts we have received and the adoption of a spirit of temperance, moderation, abstinence, self-control and solidarity. These virtues, which have accompanied the history of humanity, summon us to a more simple and sober life, and unfailing concern for the needs of those around us. By adopting such a lifestyle, we will grow in a fraternal solidarity that seeks the common good and avoids the individualism and egocentrism that serve only to generate hunger and social inequality. Such a lifestyle will enable us to cultivate a healthy relationship with ourselves, with our brothers and sisters, and with the environment in which we live.

[MESSAGE ON THE OCCASION OF WORLD FOOD DAY, 16.10.2019]

2.5 Protestant Ministers, Authors & Theologians

Martin Luther (1483 – 1546)

It is right to fast frequently in order to subdue and control the body. For when the stomach is full, the body does not serve for preaching, for praying, or studying, or for doing anything else that is good. Under such circumstances, God's Word cannot remain. But one should not fast with a view to meriting something by it as by a good work.

[L. BAAB, IN "FASTING: SPIRITUAL FREEDOM BEYOND OUR APPETITE" P. 60].

But then care must be taken, lest out of this freedom [from fasting and abstinence] there grows a lazy indifference about killing the wantonness of the flesh; for the roguish [son of] Adam is exceedingly tricky in looking for permission for himself, and in pleading the ruin of the body or of the mind; so some men jump right in and say it is neither necessary nor commanded to fast or to mortify the flesh, and are ready to eat this and that without fear, just as if they had for a long time had much experience of fasting, although they have never tried it.

[A TREATISE ON GOOD WORKS, XXI]

And this is the first and highest work of God in us and the best training, that we cease from our works, that we let our reason and will be idle, that we rest and commend ourselves to God in all things, especially when they seem to be spiritual and good.

After this comes the discipline of the flesh, to kill its gross, evil lust, to give it rest and relief. This we must kill and quiet with fasting, watching and labor, and from this we learn how much and why we shall fast, watch and labor. There are, alas! many blind men, who practice their castigation, whether it be fasting, watching or labor, only because they think these are good works, intending by them to gain much merit. Far blinder still are they who measure their fasting not only by the quantity or duration, as these do, but also by the nature of the food, thinking that it is of far greater worth if they do not eat meat, eggs or butter ...

I will here say nothing of the fact that some fast in such a way that they none the less drink themselves full; some fast by eating fish and other foods so lavishly that they would come much nearer to fasting if they ate meat, eggs and butter, and by so doing would obtain far better results from their fasting. For such fasting is not fasting, but a mockery of fasting and of God

[A TREATISE ON GOOD WORKS, XVII, XIX].

Ulrich Zwingli (1484 – 1531)

In a word, if you will fast, do so; if you do not wish to eat meat, eat it not; but leave Christians a free choice in the matter. You who are an idler should fast often, should often abstain from foods that make you lustful. But the labourers' lusts pass away at the hoe and plough in the field.

[THE LATIN WORKS AND THE CORRESPONDENCE OF HULDERICH ZWINGLI, P. 87].

Indeed, I say that it is a good thing for a man to fast, if he fasts as fasts are taught by Christ: Matthew vi., 16, and Isaiah 58:6. But show me on the authority of the Scriptures that one cannot fast with meat.

[THE LATIN WORKS AND THE CORRESPONDENCE OF HULDERICH ZWINGLI, P. 88]

William Tyndale (c. 1494–1536)

Fasting is to abstain from surfeiting, or overmuch eating, from drunkenness, and care of the world (as thou mayest read Luke xxi.) and the end of fasting is to tame the body that the Spirit may have a free course to God, and may quietly talk with God. For overmuch eating and drinking, and care of worldly business, press down the spirit, choke her and tangle her that she cannot lift up herself to God. Now he that fasteth for any other intent than to subdue the body, that the spirit may wait on God, and freely exercise herself in the things of God, the same is blind, and wotteth [knows] not what he doth, erreth and shooteth at a wrong mark, and his intent and imagination is abominable in the sight of GOD.

[WILLIAM TYNDALE]

John Calvin (1509 – 1564)

A holy and lawful fast has three ends in view. We use it either to mortify and subdue the flesh, that it may not wanton, or to prepare the better for prayer and holy meditation; or to give evidence of humbling ourselves before God, when we would confess our guilt before him.

[INSTITUTES OF THE CHRISTIAN RELIGION, CH. 12.15].

In regard, then, to the discipline of which we now treat, whenever supplication is to be made to God on any important occasion, it is befitting to appoint a period for fasting and prayer. Thus when the Christians of Antioch laid hands on Barnabas and Paul, that they might the better recommend their ministry, which was of so great importance, they joined fasting and prayer (Acts 13:3). Thus these two apostles afterwards, when they appointed ministers to churches, were wont to use prayer and fasting (Acts 14:23). In general, the only object which they had in fasting was to render themselves more alert and disencumbered for prayer.

[INSTITUTES OF THE CHRISTIAN RELIGION, CH. 12.16].

But that there may be no error in the name, let us define what fasting is; for we do not understand by it simply a restrained and sparing use of food, but something else. The life of the pious should be tempered with frugality and sobriety, so as to exhibit ... a kind of fasting during the whole course of life. But there is another temporary fast, when we retrench somewhat from our accustomed mode of living, either for one day or a certain period, and prescribe to ourselves a stricter and severer restraint in the use of that ordinary food.
This consists in three things — viz. the time, the quality of food, and the sparing use of it.

[INSTITUTES OF THE CHRISTIAN RELIGION, CH. 12.18].

The first thing is constantly to urge the injunction of Joel, "Rend your heart, and not your garments" [Joel 2:13]; that is, to remind the people that fasting in itself is not of great value in the sight of God, unless accompanied with internal affection of the heart, true dissatisfaction with sin and with one's self, true humiliation, and true grief, from the fear of God . . .

[INSTITUTES OF THE CHRISTIAN RELIGION, CH. 12.19].

John Knox (c. 1514 – 1572)

To this private fasting, which standeth chiefly in a temperate diet, and in powering further of our secret thoughts and necessities before God, can be prescribed no certain rule, certain time, nor certain ceremonies ; but as the Causes and occasions why that exercise is used are divers (yea, so divers that seldom it is that many at ones are moved with one cause), so are diet, time, together with all other circumstances, required to such Fasting, put in the liberty of them that use it.

To this Fasting, we have been faithfully and earnestly exhorted by our Preachers, as oft as the Scriptures, which they entreated, offered unto them occasion. And we doubt not but the godly within this Realm have used the same as necessity craved...

[A TREATISE ON FASTING, P. 172].

John Bunyan (1628 – 1688)

Many more examples of this kind might be produced out of the Old Testament; but these may suffice to show that fasting was a duty often practised by the people of God, and by holy men under the law of Moses. And the gospel recommends it, from the beginning to the end, by the examples of Christ and John the Baptist, of Peter, Paul, and the rest of the apostles, as well as by their counsel and exhortations; nothing is more frequently inculcated than this duty of fasting throughout the writings of the New Testament; and, without all doubt, it is now as requisite as ever it was, since we are liable to the same infirmities, exposed to the same temptations and beset with the same dangers as the former Christians were; against all which evils fasting is the proper remedy.

[THE PILGRIM'S PROGRESS].

George Fox (1624 – 1691)

The true fast [is that] which breaks the bonds of iniquity, and deals the bread to the hungry, brings the poor that are cast out to his own house, and when he sees any naked he covers them, and hides not himself from his own flesh; here is the true fast which separates

...Therefore, all God's people are to keep the true fast of the Lord [fast] from debate and strife and the fists of wickedness; that "fast that breaks the bands of wickedness, undoes every heavy burden, breaks every yoke, lets the oppressed go free, deals bread to the hungry, clothes the naked, and brings the poor that are cast out to his house." Everyone that keeps this true fast, their health shall grow; and when they call, the Lord will hear them; "he will be their guide continually, satisfy their souls in drought, make their bones fat, and they shall be like a watered garden, and like a spring of water, whose waters fail not.".

[A DECLARATION CONCERNING FASTING, AND THE PRAYER THAT GOD ACCEPTS]

Matthew Henry (1662 – 1714)

Almsgiving, prayer, and fasting, are three great Christian duties--the three foundations of the law, say the Arabians: by them we do homage and service to God with our three principal interests; by prayer with our souls, by fasting with our bodies, by alms-giving with our estates ...

Fasting and prayer are proper means for the bringing down of Satan's power against us, and the fetching in of divine power to our assistance. Fasting is of use to put an edge upon prayer; it is an evidence and instance of humiliation which is necessary in prayer, and is a means of mortifying some corrupt habits, and of disposing the body to serve the soul in prayer. When the devil's interest in the soul is confirmed by the temper and constitution of the body, fasting must be joined with prayer, to keep under the body.

[COMMENTARY ON THE WHOLE BIBLE, VOL. V, P. 109].

Jonathan Edwards (1703 – 1758)

Under special difficulties, or when in great need of, or great longings after, any particular mercy, for yourself or others, set apart a day for secret prayer and fasting by yourself alone; and let the day be spent, not only in petitions for the mercies you desire, but in searching your heart, and in looking over your past life, and confessing your sins before God, not as it wont to be done in public prayer, but by a very particular rehearsal before God of the sins of your past life, from your childhood hitherto, before and after conversion, with the circumstances and aggravations attending them, and spreading all the abominations of your heart very particularly, and fully as possible, before him.

[THE WORKS OF JONATHAN EDWARDS: VOLUME I, P. 67].

John Wesley (1703 – 1791)

Bear up the hands that hang down, by faith and prayer; support the tottering knees. Have you any days of fasting and prayer? Storm the throne of grace and persevere therein, and mercy will come down.

[TRACTS AND LETTERS ON VARIOUS SUBJECTS, P. 340].

A fifth and more weighty reason for fasting is that it is a help to prayer; particularly when we set apart larger portions of time for private prayer. Then especially it is that God is often pleased to lift up the souls of his servants above all the things of earth, and sometimes to rapt them up, as it were, into the third heaven. And it is chiefly as it is a help to prayer that it has so frequently been found a means in the hand of God of confirming and increasing ... seriousness of spirit, earnestness, sensibility, and tenderness of conscience; deadness to the world and consequently the love of God and every holy and heavenly affection

[SERMONS ON SEVERAL OCCASIONS, P. 249].

I desired as many as could to join together in fasting and prayer, that God would restore the spirit of love and of a sound mind to the poor deluded rebels in America. Is not the neglect of this plain duty (I mean, fasting) ranked by our Lord with almsgiving and prayer, one general occasion of deadness among Christians? Can anyone willingly neglect it, and be guiltless?

[JOURNAL OF JOHN WESLEY, P. 104].

Therefore, on this ground also, every wise man will refrain his soul, and keep it low; will wean it more and more from all those indulgences of the inferior appetites, which naturally tend to chain it down to earth, and to pollute as well as debase it. Here is another perpetual reason for fasting; to remove the food of lust and sensuality, to withdraw the incentives of foolish and hurtful desires, of vile and vain affections.

[SERMON 27."UPON OUR LORD'S SERMON ON THE MOUNT", P. 348].

Joseph Smith Jr (1805 –1844)

Also, I give unto you a commandment that ye shall continue in prayer and fasting from this time forth.

DOCTRINE AND COVENANTS 88:76

And on this day thou shalt do none other thing, only let thy food be prepared with singleness of heart that thy fasting may be perfect, or, in other words, that thy joy may be full.

[DOCTRINE AND COVENANTS 59:13]

To the Reorganized Church of Jesus Christ of Latter Day Saints, throughout the world, Greeting:

It is thought to be wisdom that there should be a day of fasting and prayer observed, before the sitting of the ensuing annual conference; a day in which the church may render thanksgiving and praise to the Lord, for bounteous blessings already bestowed; and a day in which prayer and supplication may be made for the special blessings of watch care and freedom from the influence of evil spirits direction; and guidance in the spiritual and temporal affairs of the church; the opening of effectual doors for the preaching of the word and the sending of laborers into the field, and for deliverance of those afflicted, from sickness and mental bondage; it is therefore considered by us, that Sunday, March 28, 1875, be appointed such day of fasting and prayer; and that the several branches of the church are hereby requested to observe that day in appropriate service.

Presidents of districts and branches are requested to notify their several charges, so far as practicable, and see that a due respect is accorded to this request for prayer.

HISTORY OF THE CHURCH OF JESUS CHRIST OF LATTER DAY SAINTS: 1873-1890, P. 94

The Principle of Fasts Defined:
Let this be an ensample to all saints, and there will never be any lack for bread: When the poor are starving, let those who have, fast one day and give what they otherwise would have eaten to the bishops for the poor, and every one will abound for a long time; and this is one great and important principle of fasts approved of the Lord. And so long as the saints will all live to this principle with glad hearts and cheerful countenances they will always have an abundance.

[JOSEPH SMITH, HISTORY OF THE CHURCH, VOL. 7: CH. 30, P.413]

Charles G. Finney (1792-1866)

I used to spend a great deal of time in prayer; sometimes, I thought, literally praying without ceasing. I also found it very profitable, and felt very much inclined to hold frequent days of private fasting. On those days I would seek to be entirely alone with God, and would generally wander off into the woods, or get into the meeting house, or somewhere away entirely by myself.

Sometimes I would pursue a wrong course in fasting, and attempt to examine myself according to the ideas of self-examination then entertained by my minister and the church. I would try to look into my own heart, in the sense of examining my feelings; and would turn my attention particularly to my motives, and the state of my mind.

When I pursued this course, I found invariably that the day would close without any perceptible advance being made. Afterwards I saw clearly why this was so. Turning my attention, as I did, from the Lord Jesus Christ, and looking into myself, examining my motives and feelings, my feelings all subsided of course.

But whenever I fasted, and let the Spirit take His own course with me, and gave myself up to let Him lead and instruct me, I universally found it in the highest degree useful. I found I could not live without enjoying the presence of God; and if at any time a cloud came over me, I could not rest, I could not study, I could not attend to anything with the least satisfaction or benefit, until the medium was again cleared between my soul and God.

[MEMOIRS OF REV. CHARLES G. FINNEY, P. 35]

Judicious fasting greatly aids the mind in gaining an ascendance over the bodily appetites and passions.

[LECTURE XXXIV, NATIONAL FAST DAY, MAY 14, 1841]

Persons in fasting should always guard against a self-righteous state of mind. Self-righteous fasting is worse than no fasting at all.

LECTURE XXXIV, NATIONAL FAST DAY, MAY 14, 1841

Hannah Whitall Smith (1832 – 1911)

The fast we have chosen has been to afflict our souls, to bow down our heads as bulrushes, and to sit in sackcloth and ashes; and, as a consequence, instead of our bones being made fat, and our souls refreshed like a watered garden, we have found only leanness, and thirst, and misery. Our own fasts, no matter how fervently they may be carried on, nor how many groans and tears may accompany them can never bring us anything else.

Now let us try God's fast. Let us lay aside all care for ourselves, and care instead for our needy brothers and sisters. Let us stop trying to do something for our own poor miserable self-life, and begin to try to do something to help the spiritual lives of others. Let us give up our hopeless efforts to find something in ourselves to delight in, and delight ourselves only in the Lord and in His service. And if we will but do this, all the days of our misery will be ended.

[GOD OF ALL COMFORT, CHAPTER 10]

No soul can be really at rest until it has given up all dependence on everything else and has been forced to depend on the Lord alone. As long as our expectation is from other things, nothing but disappointment awaits us. Feelings may change, and will change with our changing circumstances; doctrines and dogmas may be upset; Christian work may come to naught; prayers may seem to lose their fervency; promises may seem to fail; everything that we have believed in or depended upon may seem to be swept away, and only God is left, just God, the bare God, if I may be allowed the expression; simply and only God.

[THE GOD OF ALL COMFORT, CH. 17].

Ellen G. White (1827 – 1915)

The true fasting which should be recommended to all, is abstinence from every stimulating kind of food, and the proper use of wholesome, simple food, which God has provided in abundance. Men need to think less about what they shall eat and drink of temporal food, and much more in regard to the food from heaven, that will give tone and vitality to the whole religious experience.

[COUNSELS ON DIET AND FOODS, LETTER 73].

The fire you kindle in your stomach is making your brain like a heated furnace ... Your animal passions should be starved, not pampered and fed. The congestion of blood in the brain is strengthening the animal instincts and weakening spiritual powers.

[COUNSELS ON DIET AND FOODS, PHYSIOLOGY OF DIGESTION, LETTER 142].

Andrew Murray (1828 – 1917)

Prayer is the reaching out after God and the unseen; fasting, the letting go of all that is of the seen and temporal ... fasting helps to express, to deepen, and to confirm the resolution that we are ready to sacrifice anything, to sacrifice ourselves, to attain what we seek for the kingdom of God.

[WITH CHRIST IN THE SCHOOL OF PRAYER, LESSON 13].

The faith that can overcome such stubborn resistance as you have just seen in this evil spirit, Jesus tells them, is not possible except to men living in very close fellowship with God, and in very special separation from the world--in prayer and fasting. And so He teaches us two lessons in regard to prayer of deep importance. The one, that faith needs a life of prayer in which to grow and keep strong. The other, that prayer needs fasting for its full and perfect development.

[WITH CHRIST IN THE SCHOOL OF PRAYER, LESSON 13].

Evelyn Underhill (1875 – 1941)

The true asceticism is a gymnastic not of the body but of the mind. It involves training in the art of recollection; the concentration of thought, will, and love upon the eternal realities which we commonly ignore ...

It means hard work; mental and moral discipline of the sternest kind. The downward drag is incessant, and can be combatted only by those who are clearly aware of it, and are willing to sacrifice lower interests and joys to the demands of the spiritual life.

[THE ESSENTIALS OF MYSTICISM, P. 15]

C. S. Lewis (1898 – 1963)

Fasting asserts the will against the appetite – the reward being self-mastery and the danger pride: involuntary hunger subjects appetites and will together to the Divine Will, furnishing an occasion for submission and exposing us to the danger of rebellion. But the redemptive effect of suffering lies chiefly in its tendency to reduce the rebel will.

Ascetic practices, which in themselves strengthen the will, are only useful in so far as they enable the will to put its own house (the passions) in order, as a preparation for offering the whole man to God. They are necessary as a means; as an end, they would be abominable, for in substituting will for appetite and there stopping, they would merely exchange the animal self for the diabolical self.

[THE PROBLEM OF PAIN. P. 112].

The contemptuous way in which you spoke of gluttony as a means of catching souls, in your last letter, only shows your ignorance. One of the great achievements of the last hundred years [by Satan] has been to deaden the human conscience on that subject, so that by now you will hardly find a sermon preached or a conscience troubled about it in the whole length and breadth of Europe.

[THE SCREWTAPE LETTERS, P. 87].

If you look for truth, you may find comfort in the end; if you look for comfort, you will not get either comfort or truth, only soft soap and wishful thinking to begin, and in the end, despair.

[MERE CHRISTIANITY, P. 32].

Good and evil both increase at compound interest. That is why the little decisions you and I make every day are of such infinite importance. The smallest good act today is the capture of a strategic point from which, a few months later, you may be able to go on to victories you never dreamed of.

[MERE CHRISTIANITY, 132].

Ole Kristian Hallesby (1879 – 1961)

Fasting is not confined to abstinence from eating and drinking. Fasting really means voluntary abstinence for a time from various necessities of life, such as food, drink, sleep, rest, association with people and so forth. The purpose of such abstinence for a longer or shorter period of time is to loosen to some degree the ties which bind us to the world of material things and our surroundings as a whole, in order that we may concentrate all our spiritual powers upon the unseen and eternal things.

[PRAYER, P. 113].

Martin Luther King, Jr. (1929 - 1968)

That Monday I went home with a heavy heart, I was weighed down by a terrible sense of guilt, remembering that on two or three occasions I had allowed myself to become angry and indignant. I had spoken hastily and resentfully. Yet I knew that this was no way to solve a problem. 'You must not harbor anger,' I admonished myself. 'You must be willing to suffer the anger of the opponent, and yet not return anger. You must not become bitter. No matter how emotional your opponents are, you must be calm.'"

[CLAYBORNE CARSON. THE AUTOBIOGRAPHY OF MARTIN LUTHER KING, JR.]

While I lay in that quiet front bedroom, I began to think of the viciousness of people who would bomb my home. I could feel the anger rising when I realized that my wife and baby could have been killed. I was once more on the verge of corroding hatred. And once more I caught myself and said: 'You must not allow yourself to become bitter'."

[CLAYBORNE CARSON, THE AUTOBIOGRAPHY OF MARTIN LUTHER KING, JR.]

Martyn Lloyd-Jones (1899-1981)

Fasting should really be made to include abstinence from anything which is legitimate in and of itself for the sake of some special spiritual purpose. There are many bodily functions which are right and normal and perfectly legitimate, but which for special peculiar reasons in certain circumstances should be controlled. That is fasting. There, I suggest, is a kind of general definition of what is meant by fasting.

[STUDIES IN THE SERMON ON THE MOUNT, VOLUME 2].

This word fasting is not in all the ancient manuscripts, but it implies not only literal, physical fasting, but concentration. The value of fasting is that it enables you to give your undivided attention to a subject.

[REVIVAL, P. 19]

Arthur Wallis (1922–1988)

Fasting is important, more important perhaps, than many of us have supposed . . . when exercised with a pure heart and a right motive, fasting may provide us with a key to unlock doors where other keys have failed; a window opening up new horizons in the unseen world; a spiritual weapon of God's provision, mighty, to the pulling down of strongholds. [

[GOD'S CHOSEN FAST, P. 9].

Fasting, then, is a divine corrective to the pride of the human heart. It is a discipline of the body with a tendency to humble the soul.

[GOD'S CHOSEN FAST, P. 48].

Fasting is calculated to bring a note of urgency and [persistence] into our praying, and to give force to our pleas in the court of heaven.

[GOD'S CHOSEN FAST, P. 55].

Bill Bright (1921-2003)

Fasting is also a primary means of restoration. By humbling our souls, fasting releases the Holy Spirit to do His special work of revival in us. This changes our relationship with God forever, taking us into a deeper life in Christ and giving us a greater awareness of God's reality and presence in our lives.

[RELEASING GOD'S POWER THROUGH FASTING]

Just fast one moment at a time. Remember, you're fasting to seek God's face. Humble yourself. I encourage an individual to realize Jesus not only did it himself, but also commanded us to do what He did.

[RELEASING GOD'S POWER THROUGH FASTING]

Dallas Willard (1935 –2013)

The aim of disciplines in the spiritual life--and,
specifically, in the following of Christ--is the transformation
of the total state of the soul. It is the renewal of the whole
person from the inside, involving differences in thought,
feeling and character that may never be manifest in outward
behavior at all. This is what Paul has in mind when he speaks
of putting off the "old man" and putting on the new, "renewed
to resemble in knowledge the one who created us..."
(Colossians 3:10).

["SPIRITUAL DISCIPLINES, SPIRITUAL FORMATION & THE RESTORATION OF THE SOUL"]

Fasting, another one of the central disciplines, retrains us
away from dependence upon the satisfaction of desire and
makes the kingdom of God a vital factor in our concrete
existence. It is an indispensable application of what Jesus
called the cross. In the simplest of terms, the cross means not
doing or getting what you want. And of course, from the
merely human viewpoint getting what one wants is
everything. ...

We learn that God meets our needs in his own ways. There are "words of God" other than "bread" or physical food, and these are capable of directly sustaining our bodies along with our whole being. (Deut. 8:3-5, Matt. 4:4, John 4:32-34)

Fasting liberates us, on the basis of experience, into the abundance of God. The effects of this for the reordering of our soul are vast. Christian practitioners through the ages have understood that to fast well brought one out from under domination of desire and feeling generally, not just in the area of food.

["Spiritual Disciplines, Spiritual Formation & the Restoration of the Soul"]

As with prayer, there is no particular value in fasting for its own sake. Fasting is practiced for greater ends than itself. It clears the mind and helps us to concentrate on a specific subject, allowing us to subordinate our bodies' needs to our spiritual need for God. Fasting can also be specifically helpful in preparing us for a special event, or in seeking guidance from God. It helps us to control our appetites before they are given the chance to control us.

[The Mentored Life, p. 47]

Elisabeth Elliot (1926 – 2015)

There is little understanding today of the real purpose of hermits and anchorites. While there were undoubtedly some who thought to buy their way to heaven by crucifying the flesh, the true effectiveness was based on their willingness to serve by giving themselves wholly to prayer and contemplation. This involves sacrifice of one kind or another, today as yesterday. Hermits and anchorites chose solitude, poverty, withdrawal from the world, fasting.

[DISCIPLINE: THE GLAD SURRENDER, P. 46]

Richard J. Foster (1942 -)

The first truth that was revealed to me in my early experiences in fasting was my lust for good feelings. It is certainly not a bad thing to feel good, but we must be able to bring that feeling to an easy place where it does not control us.

[Freedom of Simplicity: Finding Harmony in a Complex World. p 164-65]

In a culture where the landscape is dotted with shrines to the Golden Arches and an assortment of Pizza Temples, fasting seems out of place, out of step with the times. In fact, fasting has been in general disrepute both in and outside the Church for many years.

[The Celebration of Discipline, p. 47].

God has given us the Disciplines of the spiritual life as a means of receiving his grace ... This is the way it is with the Spiritual Disciplines — they are a way of sowing to the Spirit. The Disciplines are God's way of getting us into the ground; they put us where he can work within us and transform us. By themselves the Spiritual Disciplines can do nothing; they can only get us to the place where something can be done.

[CELEBRATION OF DISCIPLINE: THE PATH TO SPIRITUAL GROWTH. P. 7].

Fasting reminds us that we are sustained by every word that proceeds from the mouth of God (Matt. 4:4). Food does not sustain us; God sustains us...Therefore, in experiences of fasting, we are not so much abstaining from food as we are feasting on the word of God.

[CELEBRATION OF DISCIPLINE: THE PATH TO SPIRITUAL GROWTH, P. 55]

Fasting is one expression of our struggle. Fasting is the voluntary denial of a normal function for the sake of intense spiritual activity. It is a sign of our seriousness and intensity. When we fast, we are intentionally relinquishing the first right When we fast, we are intentionally relinquishing the first right given to the human family in the Garden—the right to eat. We say no to food because we are intent upon others receiving a far greater nourishment. We are committed to breaking every yoke and setting the captives free. Our fasting is a sign that nothing will stop us in our struggle on behalf of the broken and oppressed.

[PRAYER: FINDING THE HEART'S TRUE HOME. P. 226]

John Piper (1946-)

Do you have a hunger for God? If we don't feel strong desires for the manifestation of the glory of God, it is not because we have drunk deeply and are satisfied. It is because we have nibbled so long at the table of the world. Our soul is stuffed with small things, and there is no room for the great. If we are full of what the world offers, then perhaps a fast might express, or even increase, our soul's appetite for God. Between the dangers of self-denial and self-indulgence is the path of pleasant pain called fasting.

[A HUNGER FOR GOD: DESIRING GOD THROUGH FASTING AND PRAYER, BACK COVER].

We easily deceive ourselves that we love God unless our love is frequently put to the test .... This is one way that fasting serves all our acts of love to God. It keeps the preferring faculty on alert and sharp. It does not let the issue rest. It forces us to ask repeatedly: do I really hunger for God? ... Or have I begun to be content with his gifts?

[A HUNGER FOR GOD: DESIRING GOD THROUGH FASTING AND PRAYER, PP. 21-22].

John Ortberg (1957-)

Oddly enough, people who constantly have every appetite gratified from childhood on become the least capable of gratitude. To become grateful, I must learn that I can handle disappointment and delayed gratification with grace and perseverance. This is why practices such as fasting and simplicity are such powerful tools for transformation. The experience of frustration and disappointment is irreplaceable in the development of a grateful heart.

[LOVE BEYOND REASON].

Disciplines of engagement involve my intentionally doing certain things. Worship, study, fellowship, and giving are all disciplines of engagement. By contrast, disciplines of abstinence involve my intentionally refraining from doing things. These include practices such as fasting, solitude, and silence.

[THE LIFE YOU'VE ALWAYS WANTED: SPIRITUAL DISCIPLINES FOR ORDINARY PEOPLE].

We live in a world that invites us to fall in love with something new every day. New products, new hobbies, new culinary sensations, and new entertainments cry out for our attention. Yet, in the midst of this cacophony of voices, God speaks to us and invites us to love his law. God does not scream his invitation; he simply sets before us the richness of his law and invites us to hear, learn, and grow to cherish the words of life and truth that his people have loved for millennia.

[TEACHING THE HEART OF THE OLD TESTAMENT, P. 141].

We can use our wills to override our habits for a few minutes, but our habits will always beat willpower alone in the long run. Deep change takes more than willpower. It requires God renewing our minds. It requires surrender.

[THE ME I WANT TO BE: BECOMING GOD'S BEST VERSION OF YOU, P. 50].

2.6 Additional Christian Sources

Meister Eckhart (1260 – 1327)

O Almighty and Merciful Creator and Good Lord, be merciful to me for my poor sins, and help me that I may overcome all temptations and shameful lusts, and may be able to avoid utterly, in thought and deed, what Thou forbiddest, and give me grace to do and to hold all that Thou hast commanded. Help me to believe, to hope, and to love, and in every way to live as Thou willest, as much as Thou willest, and what Thou willest.

[LIGHT, LIFE, AND LOVE].

... free thy self from all that is contingent, entangling, and cumbersome and direct thy mind always to gazing upon God in thy heart with a steadfast look that never wavers: as for other spiritual exercises— fasting, watching and prayer— direct them all to this one end, and practise them so far as they may be helpful thereto, so wilt thou win to perfection.

[MEISTER ECKHART'S SERMONS – P. 51]

Thomas À Kempis (1380 – 1471)

Consider the lively examples set us by the saints, who possessed the light of true perfection and religion, and you will see how little, how nearly nothing, we do. What, alas, is our life, compared with theirs? The saints and friends of Christ served the Lord in hunger and thirst, in cold and nakedness, in work and fatigue, in vigils and fasts, in prayers and holy meditations, in persecutions and many afflictions.

[IMITATION OF CHRIST, CH 18].

Jesus has many lovers of His kingdom of heaven, but he has few bearers of His Cross. Many desire His consolation, but few desire His tribulation. He finds many comrades in eating and drinking, but He finds few hands who will be with Him in His abstinence and fasting.

[IMITATION OF CHRIST, CH. 11].

How foolish and faithless of heart are those who are so engrossed in earthly things as to relish nothing but what is carnal! Miserable men indeed, for in the end they will see to

*their sorrow how cheap and worthless was the thing they
loved.*

IMITATION OF CHRIST. CH. 22].

*There is one thing that keeps many from zealously improving
their lives, that is, dread of the difficulty, the toil of battle.
Certainly, they who try bravely to overcome the most difficult
and unpleasant obstacles far outstrip others in the pursuit of
virtue. A man makes the most progress and merits the most
grace precisely in those matters wherein he gains the
greatest victories over self and most mortifies his will.*

[IMITATION OF CHRIST, CH. 25].

*Let thy soul therefore be strong and thy will ready to fast: for
thou hast the example of many fasting together with thee. Set
before thee now one day, and tomorrow thou shalt more
devoutly add another : and thus in God's name thou shalt
 accomplish the rest. Is not so holy a fast to be deemed all
light and brief for the kingdom of God and the love of Christ?*

[MEDITATIONS & SERMONS ON THE INCARNATION, P. 114]

William Ellery Channing (1780 – 1842)

I call that mind free which masters the senses, which protects itself against animal appetites, which contemns pleasure and pain in comparison with its own energy, which penetrates beneath the body and recognizes its own reality and greatness, which passes life, not in asking what it shall eat or drink, but in hungering, thirsting, and seeking after righteousness.

[THE WORKS OF WILLIAM E. CHANNING: VOL. 4, P. 71]

Leo Tolstoy (1828 – 1910)

A man who eats too much cannot strive against laziness, while a gluttonous and idle man will never be able to contend with sexual lust. Therefore, according to all moral teachings, the effort towards self-control commences with a struggle against the lust of gluttony—commences with fasting ... Fasting is an indispensable condition of a good life, whereas gluttony is, and always has been, the first sign of the opposite—a bad life. Unfortunately, this vice is in the highest degree characteristic of the life of the majority of the men of our time.

[THE FIRST STEP, THE WORKS OF LEO TOLSTOY].

Mary Baker Eddy (1821 – 1910)

Without a fitness for holiness, we cannot receive holiness. A great sacrifice of material things must precede this advanced spiritual understanding.

[SCIENCE AND HEALTH P. 16]

Jesus said to his disciples, "This kind goeth not out but by prayer and fasting," but he did not appoint a fast. Merely to abstain from eating was not sufficient to meet his demand. The animus of his saying was: Silence appetites, passion, and all that wars against Spirit and spiritual power. The fact that he healed the sick man without the observance of a material fast confirms this conclusion.

[THE FIRST CHURCH OF CHRIST, SCIENTIST, AND MISCELLANY, PP. 339-340]

Truth will at length compel us all to exchange the pleasures and pains of sense for the joys of Soul.

[SCIENCE AND HEALTH, P. 321]

Charles Taze Russell (1852 –1916)

Fasts were intended for one of two purposes: a manifestation of repentance, or with a view to bringing the heart into closer communion with the Lord. From earliest times fasting has been recognized as a valuable adjunct to piety. ... The more intelligent people of the world practice a kind of fasting or self-denial every day they live. They have an aim in life and eat and drink in harmony therewith. ... Fasting, like baptism, may be either a mere form, injurious rather than beneficial, or it may be observed with spiritual profit.

.... All through the Gospel age, it has been appropriate that the Lord's followers fast with the true fasting of self-denial, hungering and thirsting after righteousness. We may safely conclude that all "abstaining from fleshly lusts" or desires is real fasting, the kind most approved in the Lord's sight. If any [man] will come after me, let him deny himself, and take up his cross, and follow me.

[Expanded Biblical Comments - Commentary of the Old and New Testament]

Dietrich Bonhoeffer (1906 – 1945)

Jesus takes it for granted that his disciples will observe the pious custom of fasting. Strict exercise of self-control is an essential feature of the Christian's life. Such customs have only one purpose—to make the disciples more ready and cheerful to accomplish those things which God would have done.

Fasting helps to discipline the self-indulgent and slothful will which is so reluctant to serve the Lord, and it helps to humiliate and chasten the flesh.

[THE COST OF DISCIPLESHIP, P. 169]

W. E. B. Du Bois (1868 - 1963)

When now in these days the church ...invites healthy and joyous young people ... to renounce the amusements of this world for a diet of fasting and prayer, those same young people in increasing numbers are positively, deliberately, and decisively declining to do any such thing; and they are pointing to the obvious fact that the very church that is preaching against amusement is straining every nerve to amuse them; they feel that there is an essential hypocrisy in this position of the church and they refuse to be hypocrites... What the Negro church is trying to impress upon young people is that Work and Sacrifice is the true destiny of humanity —the Negro church is dimly groping for that divine word of Faust: "Embehren sallst du, sollst entbehren." "Thou shalt forego, shall do without.

[DU BOIS ON RELIGION, PP. 24-25]

Franklin Hall (1907–1993)

Fasting being an antipleasure measure, we are not supposed to seek pleasure in it, or to even expect such, other than spiritual pleasure Because fasting has such a power in connection with the natural [physical] things being successfully accomplished when our attention is thus directed to them, we are even forbidden to call this a consecration fast. That is, if one is fasting mainly for greater success in business, or for selfish material welfare, or for healing only, or some other personal object—this is an unacceptable fast to God."

[GLORIFIED FASTING: THE ABC OF FASTING]

When a fast is undertaken it starts in the natural [physical] and ends in the spiritual. Natural things in their proper places do play a great part when consecrated to God in drawing us into the spiritual."

[QUOTED IN SPIRIT CURE: A HISTORY OF PENTECOSTAL HEALING BY JOSEPH W. WILLIAMS, P. 69]

Thomas Merton (1915-1968)

We live in a society whose whole policy is to excite every nerve in the human body and keep it at the highest pitch of artificial tension, to strain every human desire to the limit and to create as many new desires and synthetic passions as possible, in order to cater to them with the products of our factories and printing presses and movie studios and all the rest.

[THE SEVEN STOREY MOUNTAIN, P. 148].

The Holy Spirit never asks us to renounce anything without offering us something much higher and much more perfect in return... The function of self-denial is to lead to a positive increase of spiritual energy and life.

[SEASONS OF CELEBRATION, P. 113].

Howard Thurman (1899-1981)

Only in the white heat of testing and trial, is there revealed the rugged structure of the discipline that makes for real character. It is in this sense that theory and practice can never be separated. Practice is theory realizing itself. One of the tragedies of the modern liberal is the illusion that theory and practice, the ideal and the real can be separated from each other. The Hindu poet is right—"Thou hast to churn the milk, O, Disciple, if thou desirest the taste of butter."

DEEP IS THE HUNGER: MEDITATIONS FOR APOSTLES OF SENSITIVENESS,

Ezra Taft Benson (1899–1994)

Periodic fasting can help clear up the mind and strengthen the body and the spirit. The usual fast, the one we are asked to participate in for fast Sunday, is to abstain from food and drink for two consecutive meals. Some people, feeling the need, have gone on longer fasts of abstaining from food but have taken the needed liquids. Wisdom should be used, and this fast should be broken with light eating. To make a fast most fruitful, it should be coupled with prayer and meditation; physical work should be held to a minimum, and one should ponder on the scriptures and the reason for the fast."

"Do Not Despair," Ensign, October 1986

Adalbert de Vogüé (1924-2011)

*To meet other fears, perhaps I should underline that
my endeavors at fasting have not caused any reduction of
activity. I have never had to curtail my six or seven hours of
intellectual work or renounce any physical exercise. Neither
have I experienced lassitude or lessening of output at any
time.*

[TO LOVE FASTING: THE MONASTIC EXPERIENCE, P 12].

*But on the whole, the dominant impression has not been that
of a painful tension. On the contrary, I have lived the
discovery of the fast as a joyful liberation ... The regular fast,
becoming a weekday exercise all year, is for me less an effort
than a very agreeable way of life. I practice it with pleasure
so appreciating its advantages that I regret its interruptions.*

[TO LOVE FASTING: THE MONASTIC EXPERIENCE, P. 116].

... let us return from these concrete details to the essential, which is "to love fasting," as Saint Benedict says. Today's monks no longer practice it; they do not even know what it is. How could they "love" it? ... We shall practice the fast only if we love it. But to love it we need to experience its benefits, and thus we need to practice it. Happy he who breaks out of this circle, trusting in the wisdom of the Rule and trying it!

[TO LOVE FASTING: AN OBSERVANCE THAT IS POSSIBLE AND NECESSARY TODAY, AMERICAN BENEDICTINE REVIEW 35:3-SEPT. 1984. PP. 302-312].

Isaac of Nineveh, I noted, clearly indicates the relation which unites fasting to solitude and silence. At present, I will cite only a word of St. Arsenius, where this connection appears in a more discreet fashion: "If you desire that the power of God come upon you, love fasting and avoid men." Flee from men: Arsenius is above all known for this maxim, which implies taciturnity and hesychia. But to these conditions for "salvation" must be added fasting if the monk wishes that the power of God come upon him.

[ASCETICISM TODAY, PP. 121-122]

H. H. Pope Shenouda III (1923 –2012

We eat for God so that our body may gain strength to serve
God and perform our duties and responsibilities towards
others. It is also for God that we hunger, to subdue the body
lest it sin against God, to control and not be controlled bodily
desires and lusts so that they may not control our actions.
We behave in accordance with the spirit, not the body, for the
sake of our love of God, and the fellowship with His Divine
Spirit. Fasting for any other reason is rejected by God.

[THE SPIRITUALITY OF FASTING, P. 58].

Thomas Keating (1923 –2018)

Silence is God's first language; everything else is a poor translation. In order to hear that language, we must learn to be still and to rest in God. One of the signs of the night of sense is an inclination for solitude and silence; to be alone with God, even though we find no satisfaction in it.

[INVITATION TO LOVE THE WAY OF CHRISTIAN CONTEMPLATION, P. 105].

The false self is deeply entrenched. You can change your name and address, religion, country, and clothes. But as long as you don't ask it to change, the false self simply adjusts to the new environment. For example, instead of drinking your friends under the table as a significant sign of self-worth and esteem, if you enter a monastery, as I did, fasting the other monks under the table could become your new path to glory. In that case, what would have changed? Nothing.

[THE HUMAN CONDITION: CONTEMPLATION AND TRANSFORMATION].

Desmond Tutu (1931 -)

The Archbishop fasts on a weekly basis. Fasting not only helps us develop discipline and self-control but also to foster compassion, as when we fast, we experience some of the hunger that others do not choose but are forced to endure. Letting go of our focus on food, which is a preoccupation for so many, can free more time to spend on thought and prayer.

[THE BOOK OF JOY: LASTING HAPPINESS IN A CHANGING WORLD]

Sister Prudence Allen (1940 -)

There are many in formation [spiritual training] who have an inordinate desire to use the electronic media for relaxation and recreation. They feed themselves with electronic data while they cannot be satiated. This may be adjoined to a passive lifestyle, lacking moderation in food or drink. This is indeed a new portrait of gluttony.

[FORMATION IN AN ELECTRONIC AGE].

Fr. Thomas Ryan

For Catholics, the practice of fasting has, by and large, fallen off the screen, due in large measure to the minimalistic interpretation of what Church members are told fasting means: "Take only one full meal. Two smaller meals are permitted as necessary, but eating solid foods between meals is not permitted."

Should you convey that to a Muslim or Jew or Buddhist who might ask you what fasting means for Catholics, be prepared to be looked at with an uncomprehending frown and then asked, "How is that different from a normal day? Don't you normally eat one main meal and two smaller ones? Or even if you do cut down a little, why don't you call that 'reduced eating' rather than 'fasting?'"

["GIVE YOUR FASTING TWO WINGS"]

The person who fasts stands in a noble tradition. In the religious experience of humankind, fasting has always been a prelude and means to a deeper spiritual life. Failure to control the amount we eat and drink disturbs the inner order of our body- spirit. Fasting is a choice to abstain from food at certain times in order to put our attention on something more important to us than ourselves or our sensory appetites.

Our unlimited freedoms and resources have not brought us unlimited fulfillment. The time has come for the consumer society to generate its antithesis: the person who stands against the conditioned reflex, who is free not to consume, who chooses to fast because of the self-transcending meaning and values perceived.

THE SACRED ART OF FASTING: P. XI

Fasting as a religious act increases our sensitivity to that mystery always and everywhere present to us. It is an invitation to awareness, a call to compassion for the needy, a cry of distress, and a song of joy. It is a discipline of self-restraint, a ritual of purification, and a sanctuary for offerings of atonement. It is a wellspring for the spiritually dry, a compass for the spiritually lost, and inner nourishment for the spiritually hungry.

[THE SACRED ART OF FASTING, P. 163-164].

The entire tradition of monasticism bears witness that union with God usually presupposes a life of self-discipline rather than self-indulgence. Everything comes with a price tag, and a strong love is willing to pay the price. The normal path is pointed out by Jesus: "If any want to become my followers, let them deny themselves and take up their cross and follow me" (Matt 16:24).

The primary reason for asceticism is the call to liberating transcendence of the thousand little threads that form a rope to bind us, the call to become free for service in love.

[FASTING: A FRESH LOOK,]

Albert Haase

Fasting can be a painful admission that I am not free, that my life is enslaved, obsessed or addicted to external things such as food, drink, codependent relationships, sex, television, privacy and the like. It can be a stern teacher, reminding us that we have severed the most basic of relationships, the one with ourselves, and allowed our lives to spin out of control.

[COMING HOME TO YOUR TRUE SELF, P. 108].

Michelle Singletary (1958–)

But if you think you can do this 21-day financial fast on your own, you are mistaken. It's going to take discipline. The discipline of fasting forces you to turn your focus away from the things of the world — credit and shopping — and reach out to God. Fasting at its essence is about self-denial. And Lord knows there's a need these days for people to deny their desires. For it's these wanton desires that have caused financial pain for so many.

Fasting is also about obedience. Scripture gives us many examples of people who fasted. Moses fasted. Elijah fasted. David fasted. Daniel fasted. And Jesus fasted.

[THE 21-DAY FINANCIAL FAST]

3

ISLAMIC SOURCES

3.1 Fasting in Islam

Servitude & Worship (Ibadah)

In Islam, the Arabic word *ibadah* refers to the believer's attitude of servitude to the Creator, Who is the Master and to whom absolute obedience is due. The 13th-century Islamic scholar Ibn Taymiyyah defined 'ibadah as "a comprehensive noun encompassing everything that Allah loves and is pleased with – whether saying or actions, outward or inward."

And [tell them that] I have not created the invisible beings [jinn] and men to any end other than that they may [know and] worship Me. [Quran 51:56 (Asad)]

God-consciousness (Taqwa)

The Qur'an affirms that fasting is a universal principle of worship and commands Muslims to fast. The fast is strict but makes allowances for special circumstances. Its purpose is to remain consciously aware ((taqwa تقوى) of the Divine Reality, even while fully engaging in daily secular activities.

The triliteral root of taqwa, waw-qaf-ya (و ق ي), literally means to save or guard. It occurs 258 times in the Quran, in eight derived forms. [Quran Dictionary].

Taqwa has been translated as God-consciousness, self-restraint, piety, obedience, observance of duty, reverence for God, God-fearing, guarding (against evil), and righteousness. This multiplicity of translations evidences the complexity of the word and the difficulty of conveying the meaning in English.

The Quran clearly states that it is guidance for the God-conscious muttaqin and exhorts believers to be in constant awareness of God, to be muttaqin.

O you who have attained to faith! Be conscious of God with all the consciousness that is due to Him, and do not allow death to overtake you ere you have surrendered yourselves unto Him. [Quran 3:102 (Asad)].

Thus, fasting during Ramadhan, and at other times, is an essential component of a Muslim's faith. However, fasting is not limited to what a person eats, but also includes restricting what the mouth says, the eyes look at, where the feet go, what the ear listens to, and what the hands do.

So remember Me, and I shall remember you; and be grateful unto Me, and deny Me not. [Quran 2:152 (Asad)]

3.2 Quotes from the Qur'an

Fasting

And We said: "O Adam, dwell thou and thy wife in this garden, and eat freely thereof, both of you, whatever you may wish; but do not approach this one tree, lest you become wrongdoers."

[AL-BAQARAH 2:35 (ASAD)]

O YOU who have attained to faith! Fasting is ordained for you as it was ordained for those before you, so that you might remain conscious of God.

[AL-BAQARAH 2:183 (ASAD)]

... [fasting] during a certain number of days. But whoever of you is ill, or on a journey, [shall fast instead for the same] number of other days; and [in such cases] it is incumbent upon those who can afford it to make sacrifice by feeding a needy person. And whoever does more good than he is bound to do does good unto himself thereby; for to fast is to do good unto yourselves – if you but knew it.

[AL-BAQARAH 2:184 (ASAD)].

 # Ramadhan

It was the month of Ramadhan in which the Qur'an was [first] bestowed from on high as a guidance unto man and a self-evident proof of that guidance, and as the standard by which to discern the true from the false. Hence, whoever of you lives to see this month shall fast throughout it.

[AL-BAQARAH 2:185 (ASAD)].

Permitted to you, on the night of the fasts, is the approach to your wives. They are your garments and ye are their garments. Allah knoweth what ye used to do secretly among yourselves; but He turned to you and forgave you; so now associate with them, and seek what Allah Hath ordained for you, and eat and drink, until the white thread of dawn appear to you distinct from its black thread; then complete your fast Till the night appears; but do not associate with your wives while ye are in retreat in the mosques. Those are Limits (set by) Allah: Approach not nigh thereto. Thus doth Allah make clear His Signs to men: that they may learn self-restraint.

[IAL-BAQARAH 2:187 (YUSUF ALI)].

Laylat al-Qadr

BEHOLD, from on high have We bestowed this [divine writ]
on Night of Destiny. And what could make thee conceive what
it is, that Night of Destiny? The Night of Destiny is better than
a thousand months: in hosts descend in it the angels, bearing
divine inspiration by their Sustainer's leave; from all [evil]
that may happen does it make secure, until the rise of dawn.!

[AL-QADR 97:1-5 (ASADI)].

CONSIDER this divine writ, clear in itself and clearly showing
the truth! Behold, from on high have We bestowed it on a
blessed night: for, verily, We have always been warning
[man]. On that [night] was made clear, in wisdom, the
distinction between all things [good and evil] at a behest
from Ourselves: for, verily, We have always been sending [Our
messages of guidance] in pursuance of thy Sustainer's grace
[unto man]. Verily, He alone is all-hearing, all-knowing.

[AD-DUKHAN 44:2-6 (ASAD)].

[* *Laylat al-Qadr* is considered the holiest night of the year, the
night when the first verses of the Quran were revealed. It is one of
the nights of the last ten days of the month of Ramadhan.]

[Thereupon the angels called out unto him:] "O Zachariah! We bring thee the glad tiding of [the birth of] a son whose name shall be John. [And God says,] `Never have We given this name to anyone before him." [Zachariah] exclaimed: "O my Sustainer! How can I have a son when my wife has always been barren and I have become utterly infirm through old age?"

Answered [the angel]: "Thus. it is; [but] thy 'Sustainer says, `This is easy for Me -even as I have created thee aforetime out of nothing.[Zachariah] prayed: "O my Sustainer! Appoint a sign for me!" Said [the angel]: "Thy sign shall be that for full three nights [and days] thou wilt not speak unto men.

Thereupon he came out of the sanctuary unto his people and signified to them [by gestures]: "Extol His limitless glory by day and by night!"

[MARYAM 19:7-11 (ASAD)]

And [when] the throes of childbirth drove her to the trunk of a palm-tree, she exclaimed: "Oh, would that I had died ere this, and had become a thing forgotten, utterly forgotten!"

Thereupon [a voice] called out to her from beneath that [palm-tree]: "Grieve not! Thy Sustainer has provided a rivulet [running] beneath thee;and shake the trunk of the palm-tree towards thee: it will drop fresh, ripe dates upon thee.

Eat, then, and drink, and let thine eye be gladdened! And if thou shouldst see any human being, convey this unto him: `Behold, abstinence from speech have I vowed unto the Most Gracious; hence, I may not speak today to any mortal.

[MARYAM 19:23-26 (ASAD)]

Do people think that they will be left alone because they say: "We believe," and will not be tested. And We indeed tested those who were before them. And Allah will certainly make known those who are true, and will certainly make known those who are liars.

[AL-ʿANKABUT 29:2-3 (HILALI & KHAN)]

O Children of Adam! Look to your adornment at every place of worship, and eat and drink, but be not prodigal. Lo! He loveth not the prodigals.

[AL-AʿRAF 7:31 (PICKTHALL)].

Know that the life of the world is only play, and idle talk, and pageantry, and boasting among you, and rivalry in respect of wealth and children; as the likeness of vegetation after rain, whereof the growth is pleasing to the tiller, but afterward it drieth up and thou seest it turning yellow, then it becometh straw. And in the Hereafter there is grievous punishment, and (also) forgiveness from Allah [God] and His good pleasure, whereas the life of the world is but matter of illusion.

[AL-HADID 57:20 (PICKTHALL)].

On no soul doth God Place a burden greater than it can bear. It gets every good that it earns, and it suffers every ill that it earns. (Pray:) "Our Lord! Condemn us not if we forget or fall into error; our Lord! Lay not on us a burden Like that which Thou didst lay on those before us; Our Lord! Lay not on us a burden greater than we have strength to bear. Blot out our sins, and grant us forgiveness. Have mercy on us. Thou art our Protector; Help us against those who stand against faith."

[AL-BAQARAH 2:286 (PICKTHALL)].

And, behold, with every hardship comes ease.

[AL-INSHIRAH 94:5(ASAD)]

3.3 Traditions (Ahadith)

"There is no God but Allah and Muhammad is messenger of Allah."

Imam Malik ibn Anas (93–179 AH) (711–795 CE)

Yahya related to me from Malik from Abu'z-Zinad from al-Araj from Abu Hurayra that the Messenger of Allah, may Allah bless him and grant him peace, said, "Beware of wisal [to fast continuously for more than one day]. Beware of wisal." They said, "But you practise wisal, Messenger of Allah." He replied, "I am not the same as you. My Lord feeds me and gives me to drink."

[MALIK'S MUWATTA, 18:13.39].

Praise be to God

Ahmad ibn Hanbal (164–241 AH)(780–855 CE)

Abdullah ibn Amr reported: The Messenger of Allah (ﷺ)

said, "Fasting and the Quran will intercede for the servant on
the Day of Resurrection. Fasting will say: O Lord, I prevented
him from food and drink during the day, so allow me to
intercede for him. The Quran will say: O Lord, I prevented him
from sleeping during the night, so allow me to intercede for
him. Thus, they will both intercede for him."

[MUSNAD AHMAD 6589].

The Generous Qur'an

Imam al-Bukhari (194 -256 AH)(810 – 870 CE)

Ibn `Abbas used to say, "Allah's Messenger (ﷺ)

(sometimes) fasted and (sometimes) didn't fast during the journeys so whoever wished to fast could fast, and whoever wished not to fast, could do so."

[SAHIH BUKHARI 30:38]

Narrated Ibn `Abbas: The Prophet (ﷺ) never fasted a full month except the month of Ramadan, and he used to fast till one could say, "By Allah, he will never stop fasting," and he would abandon fasting till one would say, "By Allah, he will never fast."

[SAHIH BUKHARI 30:53]

Narrated Abu Huraira: Allah's Apostle (ﷺ) said, "Fasting is a shield (or a screen or a shelter). So, the person observing fasting should avoid sexual relation with his wife and should not behave foolishly and impudently, and if somebody fights with him or abuses him, he should tell him twice, 'I am fasting."

[SAHIH BUKHARI 31: 118].

Narrated Sahl: The Prophet (ﷺ) said, "There is a gate in Paradise called Ar-Raiyan, and those who observe fasts will enter through it on the Day of Resurrection and none except them will enter through it. It will be said, 'Where are those who used to observe fasts?' They will get up, and none except them will enter through it. After their entry, the gate will be closed and nobody will enter through it."

[SAHIH BUKHARI 31:120].

Narrated Abu Huraira: Allah's Apostle (ﷺ) said, "When the month of Ramadan starts, the gates of the heaven are opened and the gates of Hell are closed and the devils are chained."

[SAHIH BUKHARI 31:123].

Narrated Abu Huraira: The Prophet (ﷺ) said, "Whoever established prayers on the night of Qadr out of sincere faith and hoping for a reward from Allah, then all his previous sins will be forgiven; and whoever fasts in the month of Ramadan out of sincere faith, and hoping for a reward from Allah, then all his previous sins will be forgiven."

[SAHIH BUKHARI 31:125].

Narrated Abu Huraira: The Prophet (ﷺ) said, "Whoever does not give up forged speech and evil actions [during Ramadan], Allah is not in need of his leaving his food and drink (i.e. Allah will not accept his fasting.)"

[SAHIH BUKHARI, 31:127].

Narrated Abu Huraira: Allah's Apostle (ﷺ) said, "Allah said, 'All the deeds of Adam's sons (people) are for them, except fasting which is for Me, and I will give the reward for it.' ... By Him in Whose Hands my soul is' the unpleasant smell coming out from the mouth of a fasting person is better in the sight of Allah than the smell of musk. There are two pleasures for the fasting person, one at the time of breaking his fast, and the other at the time when he will meet his Lord; then he will be pleased because of his fasting."

[SAHIH BUKHARI, 31: 128].

He who can afford to marry should marry, because it will help him refrain from looking at other women, and save his private parts from looking at other women, and save his private parts from committing illegal sexual relation; and he who cannot afford to marry is advised to fast, as fasting will diminish his sexual power.

[SAHIH BUKHARI, 31:129]

Allah's Apostle (ﷺ) said to me, "O 'Abdullah! Have I not been informed that you fast during the day and offer prayers all the night." 'Abdullah replied, "Yes, O Allah's Apostle!" The Prophet (ﷺ) said, "Don't do that; fast for few days and then give it up for few days, offer prayers and also sleep at night, as your body has a right on you, and your wife has a right on you, and your guest has a right on you. And it is sufficient for you to fast three days in a month, as the reward of a good deed is multiplied ten times, so it will be like fasting throughout the year." I insisted (on fasting) and so I was given a hard instruction. I said, "O Allah's Apostle! I have power." The Prophet (ﷺ) *said, "Fast like the fasting of the Prophet David and do not fast more than that." I said, "How was the fasting of the Prophet of Allah, David?" He said, "Half of the year," (i.e. he used to fast on every alternate day).*

[SAHIH BUKHARI 31:196]

A man used to eat much, but when he embraced Islam, he started eating less. That was mentioned to the Prophet (ﷺ) *who then said, "A believer eats in one intestine (is satisfied with a little food) and a Kafir eats in seven intestines (eats much).*

[SAHIH BUKHARI 70:12]

God is Great

Muslim ibn al-Hajjaj (204–261 AH) (817–875 CE)

Anas (radiallahu anhu) reported that Allah's Messenger (ﷺ) said, "Take meal a little before dawn [during Ramadan], for there is a blessing in taking meal at that time."

[THE BOOK OF FASTING (KITAB AL-SAWM): 2412].

'A'isha (Allah be pleased with her) reported that the Messenger of Allah (ﷺ) used to observe i'tikaf [retreat in a mosque] in the last ten days of Ramadan till Allah called him back (to his heavenly home). Then his wives observed i'tikaf after him.

[THE BOOK OF FASTING (KITAB AL-SAWM): 2640].

Blessings of God be upon him and peace

Al-Tirmidhi (209–279 AH)(824–892 CE)

رضي الله عنه

Mus'ab bin Sa'd narrated from his father that a man said: O Messenger of Allah(ﷺ)! Which of the people is tried most severely? He said: The Prophets, then those nearest to them, then those nearest to them. A man is tried according to his religion; if he is firm in his religion, then his trials are more severe, and if he is frail in his religion, then he is tried according to the strength of his religion. The servant shall continue to be tried until he is left walking upon the earth without any sins.

WHAT HAS BEEN RELATED) ABOUT HAVING PATIENCE WITH AFFLICTIONS

I heard the Messenger of Allah (saw) saying: 'The human does not fill any container that is worse than his stomach."

[WHAT HAS BEEN RELATED ABOUT IT BEING DISLIKED TO EAT MUCH].

Ibn Babawayh (310–380 AH) (c. 923–991 CE)

O people! A month [Ramadan] has approached you laden with blessing, mercy and forgiveness; it is a month which Almighty Allah regards as the best of all months. Its days, in the sight of Almighty Allah, are the best of days, its nights are the best of nights, its hours are the best of hours. It is a month in which you are invited to be the guests of Almighty Allah and you are regarded during it as worthy of enjoying Almighty Allah's generosity. Your breathing in it is regarded as praising Almighty Allah and your sleep as adoration, and your voluntary acts of worship are accepted, and your pleas are answered.

[PROPHET'S SERMON ON RAMADAN, IN AL-AMALI, ISLAMIC CITY BULLETIN].

An-Nawawi (631–676 AH)(1233–1277 CE)

I asked the Messenger of Allah (ﷺ): "Inform me of an act which will cause me to enter Jannah [Paradise] and keep me far from Hell." He (ﷺ) replied, "You have asked me about a matter of great importance, but it is easy for one for whom Allah makes it easy." He added, "Worship Allah, associate nothing with Him in worship, offer As-Salat (the prayer), pay the Zakat, observe Saum (fasting) during Ramadan and perform Hajj (pilgrimage) to the House of Allah, if you can afford it." He (ﷺ) further said, "Shall I not guide you to the gates of goodness? Fasting is a screen (from Hell), charity extinguishes (i.e., removes) the sins as water extinguishes fire, and standing in prayers by a slave of Allah during the last third part of the night."

[RIYAD AS-SALIHIN » THE BOOK OF THE PROHIBITED ACTIONS, 18]

On the authority of Abu 'Abd ar-Rahman 'Abdullah, the son of Umar ibn al-Khattab (RA), who said: I heard the Messenger of Allah (ﷺ) say: "Islam has been built on five [pillars]: testifying that there is no god but Allah and that Muhammad is the Messenger of Allah, performing the prayers, paying the zakat, making the pilgrimage to the House, and fasting in Ramadan."

[AN-NAWAWI, FORTY HADITH, #3].

3.4 Muslim Leaders, Scholars & Theologians

When My servants ask thee concerning Me, I am indeed close (to them): I listen to the prayer of every suppliant when he calleth on Me: Let them also, with a will, Listen to My call, and believe in Me: That they may walk in the right way.

[QURAN 2:186 (YUSUF ALI)]

ʿUmar ibn Al-Khattab (c.37 BH–23 AH)(584–644 CE)

رضي الله عنه

It is reported that on the first night of Ramaḍān, ʿUmar –

Allāh would pray Maghrib, then say (to the people):
Sit down. Then he would give a small address: Verily the
fasting of this month has been made a duty upon you, and
standing in night prayer has not been made a duty upon you,
but those amongst you who can stand in prayer should do so,
for it is from the extra good deeds about which Allāh told us:
so whoever cannot stand in prayer, let him sleep on his bed.
And beware of saying: I will fast if so and so fasts and I will
stand in night prayer if so and so stands in prayer. Whoever
fasts or stands in night prayer, he must make this for Allāh. ...
Minimize any vain or false speech in the houses of Allāh
(mosques; he said this two or three times). Let none of you
fast a few days before the month (in order to avoid missing
the beginning of the month; he said this three times). And do
not fast until you see [the crescent of the new month] unless it
is overcast. If it is overcast, count [the previous month] as 30
days. Then do not break your fasts until you see the night
upon the mountain (i.e. you are sure the sun has set).

ʿABD AL-RAZZĀQ AL-ṢANʿĀNĪ, AL-MUṢANNAF- SAYINGS OF THE SALAF.

Ali ibn Abi Talib (21 B.H–40 AH)(601–661 CE)

Many persons get nothing out of their fasts but hunger and thirst, many more get nothing out of their night prayers but exertions and sleepless nights. Wise and sagacious persons are praiseworthy even if they do not fast and sleep during the nights.

[NAHJUL BALAGHA, 144]

Abdullah bin 'Umar (11 BH-74 AH)(610–693 CE)

*By Allah, if I fasted all day without eating, prayed all night
without sleeping, spent all of my wealth in the Path of Allah,
died the day I died, but had no love in my heart for those who
obey Allah, and no hatred in my heart for those who disobey
Allah, none of this would benefit me in the least.*

[ABDULLAH BIN 'UMAR]

Abdullah Ibn Mas'ud (c.27 BH-c.32 AH)(594-c.653 CE)

*A memorizer of the Quraan should be known for his long night
prayers when people are asleep, his fasting when people are
eating, his sadness when people are happy, his silence when
people are talking nonsense, and his humbleness when people
are not. He should be wise, gentle and not talk too much: he
should not be rude, negligent, clamorous, nor hot-tempered.*

[JAWZEE, SIFAAT AS-SAFWA: 1/413]

Ja'far Al-Sadiq (83–148 AH)(702–765 CE)

The Holy Prophet said, 'Fasting is a protection from the calamities of this world, and a veil from punishment of the next.' When you fast, intend thereby to restrain yourself from fleshly appetites and to cut off those worldly desires arising from the ideas of Satan and his kind. Put yourself in the position of a sick person who desires neither food nor drink; expect recovery at any moment from the sickness of wrong actions. Purify your inner being of every lie, turbidity, heedlessness and darkness, which might cut you off from the meaning of being sincere for the sake of Allah.

[THE LANTERN OF THE PATH, FASTING, 92].

Fasting kills the desire of the self and the appetite of greed, and from it comes purity of the heart, purification of the limbs, cultivation of the inner and the outer being, thankfulness for blessings, charity to the poor, increase of humble supplication, humility, weeping and most of the ways of seeking refuge in God; and it is the reason for the breaking of aspiration, the lightening of evil things, and the redoubling of good deeds. It contains benefits which cannot be counted. It is enough that we mention some of them to the person who understands and is given success in making use of fasting, if God wills.

[THE LANTERN OF THE PATH, FASTING, P. 92].

Abstinence ... consists of leaving everything which could distract you from Allah without regret, nor feeling proud about leaving it, nor waiting for relief from your renunciation, nor seeking any praise for it.

[THE LANTERN OF THE PATH, ABSTINENCE, P. 93].

Eating out of necessity is for the pure; eating as a means and provision is a support for the precautious; eating at a time of plenty is for those who trust; and eating for nourishment is for believers ... [However, there] is nothing more harmful to the believer's heart than having too much food, for it brings about two things; hardness of heart and arousal of desires. Hunger is a condiment for believers, nourishment for the spirit, food for the heart, and health for the body.

[LANTERN OF THE PATH, EATING, P. 53].

With Allah's name and for His praise

Rabi'a Basri (99 – 185 AH) (717–801 CE)

I approached Rabi'a, and she was in the mihrab, where she was praying till day, while I, in another corner, was praying until the time of dawn and I said, "How shall we give thanks for His grace given to us, whereby we spent the whole night in prayer?" She said, "By fasting tomorrow"

[M. SMITH, RABI'A, THE MYSTIC & HER FELLOW-SAINTS IN ISLAM, P. 29]

Sahl al-Tustari (203 – 283 AH) (c.818 – c.896 CE)

Sahl al-Tustari was asked, "What do you say of the man who eats once a day?" He replied, "It is the eating of the believers"- "And three times a day?" He retorted, "Tell your people to build you a trough!"

[QUOTED IN HOSPITALITY AND ISLAM: WELCOMING IN GOD'S NAME BY MONA SIDDIQUI, P. 88]

Ibn 'Abd al-Barr (368–463 AH) (978 –1071 CE)

In the Shari'a, I'TIKAF designates staying in the mosque and not going about for the sake of earning and other things nor doing what is permitted of intercourse and other things while remaining resident in the mosque.

The basis of i'tikaf linguistically means to remain constant with something. I'tikaf in the last ten days of Ramadan is sunna. It is permitted in other than Ramadan.

There is according to Malik and most of the people of Madina there can be no i'tikaf except when fasting. I'tikaf is valid on every day in which it is valid to fast. I'tikaf is invalid in every day in which fasting is invalid. It is not permitted to do i'tikaf on the day of the 'id or the days of Mina...

There is nothing wrong in writing a little in the mosque for something which he needs nor in reciting Qur'an, but there should be no buying or selling.

The person should not occupy himself with trade or goods nor any need which will distract him from dhikr and from what he is doing. While he is clinging to the mosque, there is no harm in designating someone to attend to his business.

[KITAB AL-KAFI, CH. ON FASTING]

Al-Ghazali (450–503 AH)(c. 1058–1111 CE)

In short, the cause of perdition for people is their possessive attitude toward the world; and the cause of their eagerness for things worldly lies in both the belly and the genitals; and the cause of the genital's lust is the lust of the stomach. So in reducing food intake, one finds barriers to all of these entries as they are the gateways to Hell; and in closing them, the gateways of Paradise are opened. He (ﷺ) said: "persist in knocking on the gates of Heaven with hunger."

[ABSTINENCE IN ISLAM, PP. 59-60].

The Fast of the [spiritually elevated] Elite means fasting of the heart from unworthy concerns and worldly thoughts, in total disregard of everything but God, Great and Glorious is He. This kind of Fast is broken by thinking of worldly matters, except for those conducive to religious ends, since these constitute provision for the Hereafter and are not of this lower world.

[THE MYSTERIES OF FASTING THE MONTH OF RAMADAN].

*Know, O dear readers, that there are three classes of fast. (1)
Fast of the general Muslims. It is to restrain, oneself from
eating and drinking and from sexual passion. This is the
lowest kind of fast. (2) Fast of the few select Muslims. In this
kind of fasting, besides the above things, one refrains himself
from sins of hand, feet, sight and other limbs of body. (3) Fast
of the highest class. These people keep fast of mind. In other
words, they don't think of anything else except God and the
next world. They think only of the world with the intention of
the next world as it is the seed ground for the future . . . This
highest class of people are the Prophets and the near ones of
God. This kind of fast is kept after sacrificing oneself and his
thoughts fully to God*

[ULUM-ID-DIN (THE BOOK OF RELIGIOUS LEARNING), SEC. 2].

Oh Allah

Abdul Qadir al-Jilani (470–561 AH)(1078–1166 CE)

The fasting prescribed by the religion is to abstain from eating and drinking and sexual intercourse from dawn to sunset, while spiritual fasting is, in addition, to protect all the senses and thoughts from all that is unlawful. It is to abandon all that is disharmonious, inwardly as well as outwardly. The slightest breach of that intention breaks the fast. Religious fasting is limited by time, while spiritual fasting is forever and lasts throughout one's temporal and eternal life. This is true fasting.

[SPIRITUAL FASTING, CH. 82].

The fast of truth... is preventing the heart from worshiping any other than the essence of Allah. It is performed by rendering the eye of the heart blind to all that exists, even in the secret realms outside of this world, except the love of Allah...

There is nothing worthy to wish for, there is no other goal, no other beloved in this world and in the hereafter, except Allah. If an atom of anything other than the love of Allah enters the heart, the fast of truth, the true fast, is broken. Then one has to make it up, to revive that wish and intention, to return back to His love, here and in the hereafter. For Allah says: 'Fasting is only for me, and only I give its reward'.

[THE SECRET OF SECRETS, P. 83].

Moinuddin Chishti. (530 - 627 AH) (1136 - 1230 CE)

The real definition of fasting is that man should keep closed his heart from the desire and wishes of the world and religion. Because religious desires are like the desire for houries (beautiful women) and heaven. These create a veil in between man and his Creator. When this happens then there cannot be a meeting of the slave with his Creator. And the desires of the world are the desire of status and wealth as well as sensual desires and all are like shirk (idolatry)...

Real fasting is correct when a person removes everything from his heart except Allah. It means one should not pursue knowledge of the unrelated (ephemeral) and should take away each and every kind of desire and each and every kind of fear from his heart.

[ISRAR-E- HAQIQI, PP. 21-22]

Ibn Arabi (561–638 AH)(1165–1240 CE)

Know that fasting (sawm) is both abstention and elevation. ...
It is because the fast has a higher degree than all other acts
of worship that it is called "fast" (sawm). Allah elevated it by
denying that it is like any other act of worship....
He denied its ownership to His servants although they
worship Him by it and ascribed the fast to Himself. Part of its
affirmation is that He rewards the one who is described by it
by His hand even though He connected it to Himself when He
stated that it is not like anything else.

[AL-FUTUHAT AL-MAKKIYYA, (THE MECCAN OPENINGS) CH. 71, "ON THE SECRETS
OF FASTING"].

There are two kinds of seclusion: firstly, the seclusion of the
aspirants (muridun), which consists of not associating
physically with others; and secondly, the seclusion of the
verifiers (muhaqqiqun), which consists of having no contact
with created things in one's heart: their hearts have no room
for anything other than the knowledge of God, exalted is He,
which is the witness of the Truth in the heart that results
from contemplation.

[THE FOUR PILLARS OF SPIRITUAL TRANSFORMATION, P. 34].

*Muslim related from the hadith of Sahl ibn Sa'd that the
Messenger of Allah said, "There is a door in the Garden called
the Quenching. The fasters will enter it on the Day of Rising.
None except them will enter it. It will be said, 'Where are the
fasters?' and they will enter it. When the last of them has
gone in it, it will be locked and no one else will enter it." That
is not said about any of the commanded or forbidden acts of
worship except for the fast. By "the Quenching,"*
*He made it clear that they obtain the attribute of perfection
in action since they are described by that which has no like as
we already said. In reality, the one who has no like is the
perfect. The fasters among the gnostics enter it here, and
there they will enter it with the knowledge of all creatures.*

[AL-FUTUHAT AL-MAKKIYYA, (THE MECCAN OPENINGS) CH. 71, "ON THE
SECRETS OF FASTING"].

سلام

Peace

Al-`Izz Ibn `Abd Al-Salam (577-660 AH) (1182-1262 CE)

As for fasting repelling sinful thoughts and bad behaviour, this is because if the nafs [appetites, lower self; ego-soul] is gratified or satiated, it inclines towards and directs itself to disobedience as well as bad behaviour. If it is made to feel hungry or thirsty, it will long for food and drink. The inclinations and desires of the nafs towards spirituality and to busy it with that is better than its inclination towards and desire for disobedience and lapsing into sin. This is why some of the Salaf preferred fasting over the other acts of worship. One was asked about that and he replied: 'because I would prefer Allah looking at my nafs while it is in conflict with me over food and hunger than when it is in conflict with me over disobedience to Him [after] having been satiated

[IMAM AL-`IZZ IBN `ABD AL-SALAM, MAQASID AL-SAWM, P.17.]

Jalal ad-Din Rumi (604–672 AH)(1207–1273 CE)

What hidden sweetness is found in this empty stomach! Man is
like a lute, neither more nor less: When the lute's stomach is full, it
cannot lament, whether high or low. If your brain and stomach
burn from fasting, their fire will draw constant lamentation from
your breast. Through that fire you will burn a thousand veils at
every instant–you will ascend a thousand degrees on the Way and
in your aspiration.

[THE SUFI PATH OF LOVE, DIVAN: GHAZAL 1739, P. 157].

Is not sobriety the alighting-place of every care? Is not joy banned
in anxiety? Fast, for fasting is great gain; the faster drinks the
wine of the spirit.

[MYSTICAL POEMS OF RUMI, P. 287].

Since the prophet said "Fasting is a protection," lay hold of that,
do not cast away this shield before the arrow-shooting carnal
soul.

[MYSTICAL POEMS OF RUMI, P. 230].

Be empty of stomach and cry out, in neediness, like the reed flute!
Be empty of stomach and tell secrets like the reed pen!

[DIVAN: GHAZAL 1739]

Ibn Taymiyyah (661–728 AH) (1263–1328 CE)

The night prayers of Ramadan have not been limited to a specific number (of rak'ahs*). He (the Prophet) himself (may Allah raise his rank and grant him peace) used to pray no more than 13 rak'ahs in Ramadan or any other time. However, he used to pray with long rak'ahs. When 'Umar gathered the people behind Ubayy ibn Ka'b, he (Ubayy) used to pray 20 rak'ahs with them, and then pray three rak'ahs of witr*. He used to recite less in the rak'ahs to compensate for the increased number, since that was easier for the believers than long rak'ahs. After that, some of the Salaf used to pray 40 rak'ahs, adding three for witr*. Others prayed 36 rak'ahs, adding three for witr. All of this was acceptable. Whichever of these ways a person chooses to pray in Ramadan is fine.

SHAYKH AL-ISLAAM IBN TAYMIYYAH].

[*Rak'ah is the basic unit or part of Muslim prayers; every prayer is divided into 'rak`ats'.
**Salat-ul-Witr is a non-obligatory prayer performed at night after the night-time prayer and before the dawn prayer.]

Ibn Qayyim al-Jawziah (691 AH–751 AH) (1292–1350 CE)

As for the spiritual benefits, fasting also protects the believer from evil, guides his heart to avoid possible trespassing, balances his mind, and helps him better perform other religious obligations, including observing supererogatory prayers (Arb. nafl), and reading the Qur'an and having a better understanding of it, among other benefits of nocturnal worship.

NATURAL HEALING WITH TIBB MEDICINE, MEDICINE OF THE PROPHET
(MUHAMMAD AL-AKILI), P. 254

Ahmad ibn Naqib al-Misri (702-769 AH)(1302–1367 CE)

Things One May Be Held Legally Responsible For:

Hardship... is of two types. The first is that which people are accustomed to bear, which is within the limits of their strength, and were they to continue bearing it, it would not cause them harm or damage to their persons, possessions, or other concerns. The second is that which is beyond what people are accustomed to bear and impossible for them to continually endure because they would be cut off, unable to go on, and damage and harm would affect their persons, possessions, or one of their other concerns.

Examples include fasting day after day without breaking it at night, a monastic life, fasting while standing in the sun, or making the pilgrimage on foot. It is a sin for someone to refuse to take a dispensation and insist on the stricter ruling when this will probably entail harm (`Ilm usul al-fiqh (y71), 128-33).

RELIANCE OF THE TRAVELER

I2.0 Days On Which Fasting Is Recommended. It is recommended to fast:

(1) on six days of the month of Shawwal, and that they be the six consecutive days immediately following `Eid al-Fitr

(2) on 9th and 10th of Muharram;

(3) on the full moon...days of every lunar month, which are the thirteenth and the two days that follow it;

(4) on Mondays and Thursdays;

(5) on the first nine days of Dhul Hijja;

(6) during the inviolable months, which are four: Dhul Qa'da, Dhul Hijja, Muharram, and Rajab;

(7) and on every other day, a fast described by the Prophet (Allah bless him and give him peace) as "the most beloved fast to Allah"

In general, the best month for fasting, after Ramadan and the inviolable months, is Sha'ban

It is recommended to fast on the Day of `Arafa (9 Dhul Hijja), unless one is a pilgrim present at Arafa (def:j8) when it is better not to fast. It is not offensive for such a person to fast, though it is better for him not to.

RELIANCE OF THE TRAVELER

Mawlay al-Arabi al-Darqawi (1174-1239 AH)(1760–1823 CE)

A lot of your actions have no profit for you when your heart is malignant, no matter what you do. You will have profit from a sound breast along with what Allah has obliged you to do. If you have that, then a little bit of action is enough for you. Fasting all day, praying all night, and constant 'ibada [worship] will have no profit for you if your heart is sick and you are absorbed in what Allah dislikes in you. We seek refuge with Allah from your state and the state of those like you!

[THE DARQAWI WAY, LETTER OF SHAYKH MAWLAY AL-ARABI AL-DARQAWI, PP. 109-110].

He is Allah

3.5 Additional Muslim Sources

Inayat Khan (1299–1345 AH)(1882 –1927 CE)

There are three principal wines, three principal intoxications: the intoxication of one's self, the intoxication of one's occupation, and the third intoxication which is what the senses feel every moment . . . And as a person advances in meditative life, he may arrive at that stage where . . . he will become convinced that he can exist without these three intoxications. Verily, this conviction of existing independently of these three wines, which bring man the realization of external life, is the essence of the divine message and of all religions.

[THE WAY OF ILLUMINATION, THE ALCHEMY OF HAPPINESS].

Wisdom which is like the essence of life and which is to be found within oneself can only be attained by first making the mind obedient; and this can be done by concentration. If a person's mind is not under control, how can he use it? It is one thing to learn, and another thing to make use of one's learning. It does not suffice to learn a song: that does not make a person into a singer. He must learn to produce his voice also. And so it is with intuitive knowledge. When a man has become qualified by studying for a long time and yet cannot use his knowledge, what is the good of it? There is a sufficient number of learned people; what we want today is people with master minds, those who see not only the outer life but also the life within, who draw inspiration not only from the outer life but also from the life within. Then they become the expression of that perfect Being which is hidden, hidden behind the life of variety.

[THE TEACHING OF HAZRAT INAYAT KHAN, VOL. 7, "IN AN EASTERN ROSE GARDEN"]

Muhammad Iqbal (1294–1357 AH)(1877–1938 CE)

Thy soul cares only for itself, like the camel:
It is self-conceited, self-governed, and self-willed.
Be a man, get its halter into thine hand,
That thou mayst become a pearl albeit thou art a potter's vessel ...
Fasting makes an assault upon hunger and thirst
And breaches the citadel of sensuality.
The pilgrimage enlightens the minds of the Faithful:
It teaches separation from one's home and destroys attachment to
one's native land;
It is an act of devotion in which all feel themselves to be one,
It binds together the leaves of the book of religion.
Almsgiving causes love of riches to pass away
And makes equality familiar;
It fortifies the heart with righteousness,]
It increases wealth and diminishes fondness for wealth.
All this is a means of strengthening thee:
Thou art impregnable, if thy Islam be strong.
Draw might from the litany "O Almighty One!"
That thou mayst ride the camel of thy body.

THE SECRETS OF THE SELF

Said Nursi (c.1294–1379 AH)(1877–1960 CE)

The most excellent fasting is to make the human senses and organs, such as the eyes, ears, heart, and mind, fast together with the stomach.

That is, to withdraw them from unlawful things and from trivia, and to urge each of them to their particular worship.

For example, to ban the tongue from lying, back-biting, and obscene language, thus making it fast, and to busy it with such activities as reciting the Qur'an, praying, glorifying Allah's Names, asking for Allah's blessings for the Prophet Muhammad ((ﷺ)), and seeking forgiveness for sins. And for example, to prevent the eyes looking at strangers [of the opposite sex], and the ears from hearing bad things, and to use the eyes to take lessons and the ears to listen to the truth and to the Qur'an – similarly making other organs fast too.

As a matter of fact, since the stomach is the largest factory, when it has an enforced holiday from work through fasting, the other small workshops are made to follow it easily.

[LETTERS, THE TWENTY-NINTH LETTER, SEVENTH POINT].

Malcolm X (1343–1386 AH) (1925 – 1965 CE)

The Honorable Elijah Muhammad teaches us not only the principles of Muslim belief but also the principles of Muslim practice: We practice fasting (we eat only one meal every twenty-four hours, and we abstain from all food for three days out of every month of the year . . . and we fast also during the holy month of Ramadan.

[THE END OF WHITE WORLD SUPREMACY: FOUR SPEECHES].

You find in large numbers they [Negroes] are turning toward the religion of Islam. They are becoming Muslims, believing in one God, whose proper name is Allah, in Muhammad as his apostle, in turning toward Mecca, praying five times a day, fasting during Ramadan, and all the other principles that are laid out by the religion of Islam.

[MALCOLM X: THE LAST SPEECHES, P. 43

Elijah Muhammad (1315–1395 AH)(1897–1975 CE)

FASTING takes away evil desires. Fasting takes from us filthy desires. Fasting takes from us the desire to do evil against self and our brothers and sisters. We are created of the material of goodness. Therefore, good belongs to us...and it should not be hard for us to turn to our own selves in which we were created...good.

We are approaching the month of December, in which we usually abstain from eating in the daylight hours, as the Orthodox Muslims do, [in] the ninth (9th) month of their calendar, the month of Ramadan.

I set up this for you and me, to try to drive out of us the old white slavemaster's worship of a false birthday (December 25th) of Jesus. ...

HOW TO EAT TO LIVE, VOLUME 2, P. 49

Muhammad Asad (1318–1415 AH)(1900–1992 CE)

As the Quran points out, fasting has been widely practiced at all times of man's religious history. The extreme rigour and the long duration of the Islamic fast...fulfills, in addition to the general aim of spiritual purification, a three-fold purpose: (1) to commemorate the beginning of the Qur'anic revelation which took place in the month of Ramadan about thirteen years before the Prophet's exodus to Medina (2) to provide an exacting exercise of self-discipline; (3).to make everyone realize, through his or her own experience, how it feels to be hungry and thirsty, and thus to gain a true appreciation of the needs of the poor.

[THE MESSAGE OF THE QUR'AN, PP. 38-39, NOTE 155]

Frithjof Schuon (1325–1419 AH)(1907 – 1998 CE)

Christianity rests also on the two supreme commandments, which contain "all the law and the prophets". In gnosis, the first commandment—total love of God—implies awakened consciousness of the Self, whereas the second—love of neighbor—refers to seeing the Self in what is "not-I". Likewise for the injunctions of oratio et jejunium: all Christianity depends on these two disciplines, "prayer and fasting".

Oratio et jejunium: "fasting" is first of all abstention from evil, and then the "void for God" (vacare Deo) in which "prayer"— the "remembrance of God"—is established, and which is filled by the victory already won by the Redeemer.

[THE ESSENTIAL FRITHJOF SCHUON, P. 235]

Abd al-Aziz ibn Baz (1328–1420 AH)(1910–1999 CE)

It is obligatory upon the Muslim to fast with faith and hoping for reward and not [to fast] to be seen or heard of the people or follow the customs of the people or follow his family or the people of his country. Rather, it is obligatory upon him that that which has caused him to fast be his belief that Allah has made it a duty upon him.

FATAWA REGARDING FASTING & ZAKAH

Martin Lings (1327–1426 AH)(1909 –2005 CE)

The ritual act of prostration, which is an extremity of self-effacement, is implicit in one of Muhammad's secondary names, Abd Allah, the Slave of God. Without the complete self-effacement of slavehood it is impossible to draw nigh or, in other words, without first being empty of other than God it is impossible to be filled with the ever-present Reality of His Nearness, of which the Quran says: We (God) are nearer to him (man) than his jugular vein.

[A SUFI SAINT OF THE TWENTIETH CENTURY: SHAIKH AḤMAD AL-'ALAWĪ, P. 37]

Javad Nurbakhsh (1345–1429 AH)(1926 – 2008 CE)

If a Sufi engages in external devotions and spiritual exercises, it is strictly for the purpose of disciplining the ego in an effort to resist its desires and to purify oneself inwardly. Such a Sufi understands perfectly well that God has no need of our devotions.

SUFISM TODAY

In Sufism abstinence alone is not enough to purify the self. It is true that asceticism and abstinence may give one a certain spiritual state and that, in this state, one's perception may be clarified. But if the self is likened to a dragon that by fasting becomes powerless, it is certain that when the fast is broken and enough food is eaten, the dragon will revive and, stronger than ever, go about attempting to fulfill its desires

[THE PATH: SUFI PRACTICES]

W. D. Mohammed (1352–1429 AH) (1933–2008 CE)

The great benefit of fasting is the development of self-mastery. It is hard for us to make ourselves do what we know is good for self and others because we are weak. Prayer, right thinking, and fasting help us to overcome this weakness. Fasting gives us the strength to overcome the drive of physical hunger.

Almost the whole life of the animal world is ruled over by the drive to overcome hunger ... If you can control that very powerful drive, it not only gives you the power to withstand the flesh, but it helps you in every way because everything in the universe is related. The body affects the mind, the mind affects the body, morality is affected - all these things influence each other...

By thinking on Allah's great wonders, we are kept powerful and very much alive. Our mind (the inner being) is awakened and it makes us stand up independent of the outer body. Though the outer body is crying for food, the inner being can't hear it. It has separated itself from the outer body and it is living in the world of the higher form...

BILALIAN NEWS, 1976-SEPTEMBER-24

Hossein Nasr (1352 AH–) (1933 CE–)

*Without an element of self-denial and asceticism, no religion
and therefore no human culture is possible. One must
withdraw occasionally from the full life of the senses even in
order to be able to enjoy the fruit of sensual perception.
As the Taoist saying affirms, it is the empty space of the
wheel which makes the wheel. It is only a certain degree of
restraint from the material objects of the senses that makes
even the life of the senses balanced, not to speak of making
possible an opening in the human soul for the spiritual life.
Ramadan is an opportunity for Muslims to impart a
particular focus upon cleansing one's heart, soul, spirit
through the fast.*

[ISLAMIC LIFE AND THOUGHT, P. 214,]

Khalid Abdullah Tariq Al-Mansour (1354 AH–)
(1936 CE–)

Accordingly, don't fight hunger. Rather, welcome it as an absolutely necessary step to set up a highly intense environment from which an unusual opportunity for growth often unfolds.

It is similar to smelting metallic ore to obtain desired precious metals. Unless and until you are able to raise the temperature to the designated melting point, you will never get the purified products.

WELCOME TO ISLAM, P. 200

Fethullah Gülen (1360 AH–) (1941 CE–)

Fasting may be difficult, but it provides the body with energy, activity, and resistance ... Human life is a composite of two distinct powers: the spirit and the flesh. Although they sometimes act in harmony, conflict is more usual – conflict in which one defeats the other. If bodily lusts are indulged, the spirit grows more powerless as it becomes more obedient to those lusts. If one can control the desires of the flesh, place the heart (the seat of spiritual intellect) over reason, and oppose bodily lusts, he or she acquires eternity.

[QUESTIONS & ANSWERS ABOUT ISLAM, VOLUME 2, P.22].

Muhammad Taqī ʿUthmānī (1362 AH–) (1943 CE–)

"Taqwa" means to abstain from sinning while being conscious of the greatness of Allah. In other words, to constantly remind myself that I am a slave of Allah and He is watching me, and I will have to answer in front of Him; with this in mind, when a person abandons a sin, it is called taqwa...

Just as the medicine is necessary to cure a disease, so is the abstinence from that which causes it or adds to it! Allah has made fasting obligatory in this month in order for us to acquire "taqwa," but that cannot be without the abstinence from sins. If you turn on the air-conditioner of your room, but you don't close up your windows, it will not cool your room. Similarly, if you leave the windows of sins open, your fast will not be able to give you its desired benefit.

[MUSLIM MATTERS, "WHAT FASTING DEMANDS FROM US"]

Muhammad H. al-Asi (c. 1370– AH) (c. 1951– CE)

Fasting is a moral force that fosters the growth of self-determination and willpower. It is also the catalyst for an intense intimacy with Allah (ﷻ). Simultaneously, fasting raises the concerns of man beyond his physical appetites and worldly desires.

[THE ASCENDANT QUR'AN: REALIGNING MAN TO THE DIVINE POWER CULTURE VOLUMES 2, P. 218]

No doubt, with modern investigative techniques in the functioning of the human body, the number of medical discoveries concerning the benefits of fasting is ever-increasing. But we need not anxiously place a high premium on scientific observation to rationalize the advantages of sawm (fasting), because the main object of this exercise is the human spirit, its willpower, its self-control, and a better understanding of Allah's (ﷻ) power presence in the world.

[THE ASCENDANT QUR'AN: REALIGNING MAN TO THE DIVINE POWER CULTURE VOLUMES 2, P. 219]

Amina Wadud, Ph.D (1372 AH–) (1952 CE –)

A week into the fast a new groove is reached. For me this means greater mental clarity, new insights even to some of the same intellectual concerns. Not being bogged down with much food must make a radical change in the body and the mind. For sure, fasting in Ramadan emphasizes the critical connection between body and ritual. It's not just about how one feels in the heart, the entire body participates so that whatever is recognized, is intensified. The Qur'an says, the fast teaches self-constraint. A solid month-long readjustment in basic habits brings not only awareness, but appreciation.

[No Ramadan Gloom and Doom]

Imam Zaid Shakir (1375 AH–)(1956 CE–)

Ramadan focuses our appreciation for the food and other material blessings we enjoy by allowing us to experience at a personal level the reality of deprivation. Ramadan focuses our devotion to God by facilitating heightened levels of individual devotion through couching them in a communal manifestation. Ramadan focuses our sincerity to God, for it is centered around fasting, the one act of worship it is impossible to "show off" with before other human beings, for at the end of the day, God alone knows if we are truly fasting. Ramadan, if we allow it to do so, focuses our spiritual energies by reintroducing the great blessing of the Qur'an into our lives. Finally, Ramadan focuses our attention on the centrality of charity in a righteous life by encouraging us to engage in greater acts of giving, following the way of our Noble Prophet, peace and blessings of God upon him.

RAMADAN: TIME TO GET REAL

Jamal ad-Deen Zaraboso (c.1379 AH–) (1960 CE –)

Attending to the prayers in the proper manner and on a daily basis is not an easy matter unless one truly believes in them. Abstaining from food and drink during the daytime of Ramadhan is also not easy unless the resolve to please Allah by fasting is present. The willingness to submit to Allah with respect to what He permits and forbids is a very great matter indeed. Those who want and believe in freedom — that is, free to follow their passions and desires — cannot submit to this condition. In fact, they will fight this condition with all of their might.

[COMMENTARY ON THE FORTY HADITH OF AL-NAWAWI, VOL. 2, P. 706]

Ismail Menk (1395 AH–)(1975 CE–)

The supplications made immediately after engaging in a good deed are more likely to be answered in the way we wished. The same applies when praying for others who are going through difficulty etc. before praying for ourselves. Hence when the fast comes to an end each day do not forget to pray for humanity at large! We are taught that when we pray for others, the angels ask that the same be given to us!

[Mufti Ismail Menk].

4

HINDU SOURCES

4.1 Fasting in Hindu Scripture

The Sanskrit word *tapas* has a root meaning "heat, penance, pain, suffering, mortification, etc." *Tapas* often describes ascetic practices that include fasting.

The actual Sanskrit word for fasting, *upavāsa*, literally means sitting near or close to God. This represents a purified and elevated condition which allows connection with the Divine.

Hindu scriptures exhort adherents to burn away their desires, engage in purifying sacrifices, and destroy their appetites. Fasting practices, at times, may reach extreme levels of asceticism.

4.2 Upanishads

*There, in that space within the heart, he lies—the controller
of all, the lord of all, the ruler of all! He does not become more
by good actions or in any way less by good actions or in any
way less by bad actions. He is the lord of all!. He is the ruler of
creatures! .He is the guarding of creatures! He is the dike
separating these worlds so they would not mingle with each
other. It is he that Brahmins seek to know by means of Vedic
recitation, sacrifice, gift-giving, austerity, and fasting. It is he,
on knowing whom, a man becomes a sage. It is when they
desire him as their world that wandering ascetics undertake
the ascetic life of wandering.*

[BRIHADÂRANYAKA (4:21-22) IN PATRICK OLIVELLE, P. 125].

*Fasting is preferable to (getting food from) devotees;
unsolicited food is better than fasting; begging alms is
preferable to unsolicited food; hence he shall subsist on alms.*

[SANNYASA UPANISHAD, SECOND ADHYAYA, 80].

An ascetic keen on feeding others, who accepts clothes, etc.,
and woolen garments or others as well as good clothes
undoubtedly falls (from virtue). Resorting to the ship of non-
duality he will gain liberation while living.

For restraint in speech, he shall observe silence; for control
over the body, he shall fast; for control over the mind, breath
control (pranayama) is prescribed.

A being is bound by (worldly) action; he gets liberated by
spiritual knowledge. Hence far-seeing ascetics do not perform
(worldly) action.

[SANNYASA UPANISHAD, SECOND ADHYAYA, 114-117].

4.3 Mahabharata

And they that have fasted for a month, proceed on cars drawn by swans. And they who have fasted for six nights proceed on cars drawn by peacocks. And, O son of Pandu, he that fasteth three nights upon only one meal without a second during this period goeth into a region free from disease and anxiety. And water hath this excellent property that it produceth happiness in the region of Yama.

[ROY, THE MAHABHARATA OF KRISHNA-DWAIPAYANA VYASA, P. 434].

Proceeding next to the river Karatoya, and fasting there for three nights, a man acquireth the merit of the horse-sacrifice. Even this is the injunction of the Creator himself. It hath been said by the wise, O king, that if a person goeth to the spot where the Ganga mingleth with the sea, he reapeth merit which is ten times that of the horse-sacrifice. Crossing over to the opposite bank of the Ganga, he that bathes there having resided for three nights is, O king, cleansed from all his sins.

[MAHABHARATA, BOOK 3, SECTION CLXLIX].

The man who teaches another the merit of fasts has never to suffer any kind of misery. The ordinances about fasts, in their due order, O son of Kunti, have flowed from the great Rishi Angiras. The man who daily reads these ordinances or hears them read, becomes freed from sins of every kind. Not only is such a person freed from every calamity, but his mind becomes incapable of being touched by any kind of fault. Such a person succeeds in understanding the sounds of all creatures other than human, and acquiring eternal fame, become foremost of his species.

[MAHABHARATA, BOOK 13, ANUSHASANA PARVA, SECTION CVI

There is no Sastra superior to the Veda. There is no person more worthy of reverence than the mother. There is no acquisition superior to that of Righteousness, and no penance superior to fast. There is nothing, more sacred, in heaven or earth, than Brahmanas. After the same manner, there is no penance that is superior to the observance of fasts. It was by fasts that the deities have succeeded in becoming denizens of heaven....

[MAHABHARATA, BOOK 13, ANUSASANA PARVA: SECTION, XVI].

Bhagavad Gita

A person whose mind is unperturbed by sorrow, who does not crave pleasures, and who is completely free from attachment, fear, and anger, is called an enlightened sage of steady intellect.

[BHAGAVAD GITA 2:56].

An undisciplined person, who has not controlled the mind and senses, can neither have a resolute intellect nor steady contemplation on God. For one who never unites the mind with God there is no peace; and how can one who lacks peace be happy?

Just as a strong wind sweeps a boat off its chartered course on the water, even one of the senses on which the mind focuses can lead the intellect astray

Therefore, one who has restrained the senses from their objects, O mighty armed Arjun, is firmly established in transcendental knowledge.

[BHAGAVAD-GITA 2:66-68].

The senses, the mind, and the intellect are said to be the abode of lust; with these it deludes a person by veiling the Self-knowledge. Therefore, O Arjuna, by controlling the senses first, kill this devil of material desire that destroys Self-knowledge and Self-realization.

[BHAGAVAD-GITA 3.40-41].

Those persons are yogis, who before giving up the body are able to check the forces of desire and anger; and they alone are happy.

[BHAGAVAD-GITA 5:23].

With senses, mind, and intellect under control; having liberation as the prime goal; free from lust, anger, and fear; such a sage is verily liberated.

[BHAGAVAD GITA 5:28].

Renunciation is declared in the scriptures to be of three kinds. Acts of sacrifice, charity and penance are not to be given up; they must be performed. Indeed, sacrifice, charity and penance purify even the great souls. All these activities should be performed without attachment or any expectation of result. They should be performed as a matter of duty, O son of Prtha. That is My final opinion.

Prescribed duties should never be renounced. If one gives up his prescribed duties because of illusion, such renunciation is said to be in the mode of ignorance. Anyone who gives up prescribed duties as troublesome or out of fear of bodily discomfort is said to have renounced in the mode of passion.

[*BHAGAVAD GITA 18:1*]

Sensual pleasures appear as nectar in the beginning, but become poison in the end; such pleasures are in the mode of passion.

[BHAGAVAD GITA 18:38]

4.4 Puranas

Agni Purana

O Brahmin! Those brahmins who do not worship fire get prosperity by vows, fasting, restraints and many kinds of gifts. The gods etc. who confer enjoyment and emancipation become pleased. One who has turned back from sins and lives with qualities it is known as upavasa.

[AGNI PURANA, 175:4-5, P. 493

The study of the Vedas sacrificial rites, celibacy, penance, restraint, earnestness, fasting and truth are the causes for (gaining) knowledge of the soul.

[AGNI PURANA, 376:35-36, P.1054]

The eleventh day of the lunar fortnight (Ekadashi) is for fasting. It is also the tithi for praying to Vishnu. The observance of Ekadashi vrata grants sons and wealth and atones for one's sins.

[AGNI PURANA, VRATAS 1.5.4].

Linga Purana

Yoga means union with God. The state of yoga is impossible to attain without the blessings of Lord Shiva. It needs a concentrated and focused mind. ... The state of yoga can never be attained until and unless a person has fully controlled the tendencies of sense organs. It can be achieved with the help of eight means Yama (Penance), Niyam (discipline), Aasan (Posture), Pranayam (Breath-control), Pratyahar (restraint of passion), Dharan (retention), Dhyan (concentration) and Samadhi (deep meditation).

TRANSLATION BY DR. S. P. BHAGAT

Shiva Purana

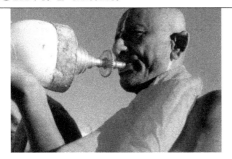

*Among all the austerities and fastings, Maha Shivaratri holds
a supreme place. It falls on the fourteenth day of the dark
lunar month of Phalgun. On this day the devotee should take
a vow to observe a fast after awakening in the morning and
finishing his daily choirs. He must observe a fast for the whole
day and night. In the night he should worship me either in the
temple or in his own home according to his convenience. He
should worship me with the help of sixteen modes of worship
(Shodasopachar). He should either chant the mantras of
Laghurudra or perform 'abhishek' during the course of
worship. ... The devotee should engage himself in my devotion
for the whole day. In the end, he should feed the brahmins
and make donation to them. A fast observed in this way gives
infinite virtues to the devotee.*

[SHIV MAHA PURANA, 4.25].

Brahmanda Purana

One shall bring Prāṇa and Apāna under control by keeping

the vital airs inter-connected with fasting. Thereafter, all the

sense-organs must be brought under control. The intellect

should be restrained within the mind and all (the sense-

organs) should be withdrawn. If this Pratyāhāra (withdrawal

of the sense-organs) is carried out, know that it is

undoubtedly the means of Liberation (mokṣa). Among the

sense-organs, the mind is terrible. The transformation of the

intellect etc. can be achieved through abstinence from food. A

person who undertakes fast attains everlasting benefit. It

should be known that fasting is a form of penance. When the

intellect and the mind are restrained, the knowledge of other

things does not arise. When all the defects are destroyed,

when the sense-organs are suppressed, the pure soul attains

the bliss of Liberation like the fire devoid of fuel.

SECTION 3 - UPODGHĀTA-PĀDA, CHAPTER 13, 138-143

There is no better fasting day than this Ekadasi of the light fortnight of the month of Margashirsha, O Yudhishthira, for it is a crystal-clear and sinless day. Whoever faithfully observes this Ekadasi fast, which is like chintaa-mani (a gem that yields all desires), obtains special merit that is very hard to calculate, for this day can elevate one from hellish life to the heavenly planets, and for one who observes Ekadasi for his own spiritual benefit, this elevates one to go back to Godhead, never to return to this material world.

[EKADASI, THE DAY OF LORD HARI]

Bhāgavata Purana

By fasting, learned men quickly bring all of the senses except the tongue under control, because by abstaining from eating such men are afflicted with an increased desire to gratify the sense of taste.

[ŚB 11.8.20]

Although one may conquer all of the other senses, as long as the tongue is not conquered it cannot be said that one has controlled his senses. However, if one is able to control the tongue, then one is understood to be in full control of all the senses.

ŚB 11.8.21

Control thyself by thy Self. Thus shalt thou overcome the world and give expression to Me. As for the one who seeks transcendence but who has not fully controlled his speech, mind, and intellect — his vows, austerities, and charity leak out like water from an unbaked jar.

A saintly person is merciful and never injures others. Even if others are aggressive he is tolerant and forgiving toward all living entities. His strength and meaning in life come from the truth itself, he is free from all envy and jealousy, and his mind is equal in material happiness and distress. Thus, he dedicates his time to work for the welfare of all others. His intelligence is never bewildered by material desires, and he has controlled his senses. His behavior is always pleasing, never harsh and always exemplary, and he is free from possessiveness. He never endeavors in ordinary, worldly activities, and he strictly controls his eating.

[ŚB 11.11.29-32].

Apamarjana Stotram

If one pleases [Vishnu], killer of [the demon] Madhu by fasting and charity, And also sees all beings equally, his soul would attain salvation.

[THE PRAYER FOR CLEANING MIND AND BODY 9].

4.5 Additional Hindu Sources

Badarayana

Knowledge having once sprung up requires no help towards the accomplishment of its fruit, but it does stand in need of something else with a view to its own origination. -- Why so?- -On account of the scriptural statements of sacrifices and so on. For the passage, 'Him Brâhmanas seek to know by the study of the Veda, by sacrifice, by gifts, by penance, by fasting' [Bri. Up. IV, 4, 22], declares that sacrifices and so on are means of knowledge, and as the text connects them with the 'seeking to know,' we conclude that they are, more especially, means of the origination of knowledge.

[THE VEDANTA SUTRAS OF BADARAYANA, III, 4, 26)].

Melpathur Narayana Bhattathiri (1560-ca.1660)

Sages have declared that, in Kali Yuga, eight deeds -

- *bathing in river Ganges;*
- *study of Bhagavad Gita;*
- *recitation of Gayatri Mantra;*
- *offer of Tulasi leaf (balsam);*
- *offer of scented clay, Gopika Chandana;*
- *worship of Saligrama (stone image);*
- *fasting on Ekadasi (11th day of each fortnight); and*
- *chanting of Thy holy names (even if done without understanding their meanings)*

all of which need little effort, lead to swift liberation through propitiating Thee. O Lord! May Thou cause me to practice these with sincerity.

[NARAYANEEYAM, DASAKAM: 92 SHLOKAM: 9].

Narasimha Sthuthi of Prahlada

Penance of silence, fasting, meditation, hearing of scriptures,

Study of sacred books, doing one's allotted duty, teaching

scriptures, Living in seclusion, muttering prayers, and

concentration of mind, Are paths that lead to salvation but,

Oh divine God, But they generally happen to be only a means

of livelihood, For those persons who have failed to conquer

their senses. And, is of no use at all to the advertising

hypocrite.

[NARASIMHA STHUTHI OF PRAHLADHA, 39].

Manava Dharma Sastra (Laws of Manu)

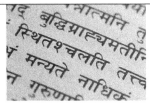

*In restraining the organs which run wild among ravishing
sensualities, a wise man will apply diligent care, like a
charioteer in managing restive horses.*

CH. II, ON THE FIRST ORDER, 88

*To a man contaminated by sensuality, neither the Vedas, nor
liberality, nor sacrifices, nor strict observances, nor pious
austerities, ever procure felicity*

CH. II, ON THE FIRST ORDER, 97

Patanjali (c. 1st – c. 2nd century CE)

Austerity [tapas], the study of sacred texts, and the dedication of action to God constitute the discipline of Mystic Union. This discipline is practised for the purpose of acquiring fixity of mind on the Lord, free from all impurities and agitations, or on One's Own Reality, and for attenuating the afflictions. The five afflictions are ignorance, egoism, attachment, aversion, and the desire to cling to life.

[PATANJALI YOGA SUTRAS, 2:1-3]

Through the purifying burning fire of tapas [exercises of discipline] all the sense organs of the body are perfected (kayendriya-siddhir) by the destruction (ksayat) of all impurities (asuddhi).

[PATANJALI, YOGA SUTRAS, II 43].

Adi Shankaracharya (788 – 820 CE}

Let my idle chatter be the muttering of prayer, my every manual movement the execution of ritual gesture, my walking a ceremonial circumambulation, my eating and other acts the rite of sacrifice, my lying down prostration in worship, my every pleasure enjoyed with dedication of myself, let whatever activity is mine be some form of worship of you.

[THE SAUNDARYALAHARI (FLOOD OF BEAUTY) P. 58:27[

Svami-Narayana (1781 –1830)

On a fast-day sleeping by day should most carefully be avoided, since by such sleep the merit of fasting is lost to men, quite as much as by sexual intercourse.

[THE SIKSHÂ-PATRÎ OF THE SVÂMI-NÂRÂYANA SECT, 80].

Swami Vivekananda (1863 – 1902)

The following are helps to success in Yoga and are called Niyama or regular habits and observances: Tapas, austerity; Svadhyaya, study; Santosha, contentment; Shaucha, purity; [and] Ishvara - pranidhana, worshipping God. Fasting, or in other ways controlling the body, is called physical Tapas.

[COMPLETE WORKS OF SWAMI VIVEKANANDA (HP788)]

Mahatma Gandhi (1869-1948)

There is no prayer without fasting. And fasting without prayer is nothing but self-torture. (Recorded under January 5, 1933; ibid., p.17.) This is 'thoroughly sound.

Here fasting has to be of the widest character possible. Fasting of the body has to be accompanied by fasting of all the senses. And 'alpahar', the meagre food of the Gita, is also a fasting of the body.

The Gita enjoins not temperance in food but 'meagerness'; meagerness is a perpetual fast. Meagerness means just enough to sustain the body of the service for which it is made.

The test is again supplied by saying that food should be taken as one takes medicine in measured doses at measured times and as required, not for taste but for the welfare of the body. 'Meagerness' is perhaps better rendered by "measured quantities." I cannot recall Arnold's rendering. A "full" meal is therefore a crime against God and man, the latter because the full-mealers deprive their neighbors of their portion. God's economy.

[SELECTED LETTERS - PART II, 56].

Fasting can help to curb animal passion, only if it is undertaken with a view to self-restraint . . . That is to say, fasting is futile unless it is accompanied by an incessant longing for self-restraint. The famous verse from the second chapter of the Bhagavad Gita is worth noting in this connection: "For a man who is fasting his senses Outwardly, the sense-objects disappear, Leaving the yearning behind; but when He has seen the Highest, Even the yearning disappears."

[MAHATMA GANDHI, AN AUTOBIOGRAPHY].

Fasting and similar discipline is, therefore, one of the means to the end of self-restraint, but it is not all, and if physical fasting is not accompanied by mental fasting, it is bound to end in hypocrisy and disaster.

[MAHATMA GANDHI, AN AUTOBIOGRAPHY].

Fasting is a potent weapon in the Satyagraha armory. It cannot be taken by everyone. Mere physical capacity to take it is no qualification for it. It is of no use without a living faith in God. It should never be a mechanical effort or a mere imitation. It must come from the depth of one's soul. It is, therefore rare.

[MAHATMA GANDHI, "INDIA OF MY DREAMS"].

Sri Aurobindo (1872 –1950)

Asceticism for its own sake is not the ideal of this yoga. but self-control in the vital and right order in the material are a very important part of it — and even an ascetic discipline is better for our purpose than a loose absence of true control. Mastery of the material does not mean having plenty and profusely throwing it out or spoiling it as fast as it comes or faster. Mastery implies in it the right and careful utilisation of things and also a self-control in their use.

BASES OF YOGA: ART OF LIVING

Sattwic Tapasya is that which is done with a highest enlightened faith, as a duty deeply accepted or for some ethical or spiritual or other higher reason and with no desire for any external or narrowly personal fruit in the action. It is of the character of self-discipline and asks for self-control and a harmonising of one's nature. The Gita describes three kinds of sattvic askesis.

First comes the physical, the askesis of the outward act; under this head are especially mentioned worship and reverence of those deserving reverence, cleanness of the person, the action and the life, candid dealing, sexual purity and avoidance of killing and injury to others.

Next is askesis of speech and that consists in the study of Scripture, kind, true and beneficent speech and a careful avoidance of words that may cause fear, sorrow and trouble to others.

Finally, there is the askesis of mental and moral perfection, and that means the purifying of the whole temperament, gentleness and a clear and calm gladness of mind, self-control and silence. Here comes in all that quiets or disciplines the rajasic and egoistic nature and all that replaces it by the happy and tranquil principle of good and virtue. This is the askesis of the sattwic dharma so highly prized in the system of the ancient Indian culture

ESSAYS ON THE GITA, P, 489

Paramahansa Yogananda (1893– 1952)

Fasting has been practiced by devotees of every religion since ancient times as an effective means of approaching God, a form of austerity to help bring the willful body and mind under control to receive the spirit of God.

PARAMAHANSA-YOGANANDA-SECOND-COMING-OF-CHRIST-VOL.1, 508

One good way to begin overcoming bad habits is to start your self-discipline with food. For example, try eating a handful of hot chili peppers, and see if you can resist the thought that they are hot. A practice some devotees in India follow is to mix everything together that they are about to eat, before they even taste it. I practiced that for a while. It was a bit strange at first, and certainly, the meal wasn't delicious with those items— sweet, pungent, bland— all tossed together! I found it helped, however, in gaining control over my palate.

[CONVERSATIONS WITH YOGANANDA BY J. DONALD WALTERS, SWAMI KRIYANANDA, YOGANANDA (PARAMAHANSA), #433]

Deep samadhi meditation is possible only when all bodily functions are stilled. Proper diet and fasting are helpful in conditioning the body for this state of quiet and interiorization. Jesus acknowledged this principle by fasting to spiritualize his body and free his mind during his forty and periodic fasting days in the wilderness.

PARAMAHANSA-YOGANANDA-SECOND-COMING-OF-CHRIST-VOL.1-

A day of fasting and introspective silence, tapping the peaceful wisdom reservoir of the soul, gives — each individual a chance to think things over and re- Sabbath is a necessary organize his life into a balanced mode. Sermons and observance for periods of silence and meditation on the Sabbath peaceful, balanced life recharge body, mind, and soul. This peace, if deeply infused into the consciousness, may last throughout the whole week, helping man to battle his restless moods, temptations, and financial worries. If the worldly person gives six days of the week to moneymaking pursuits, eating, and amusements, should he not give at least one day to the thought of God, without whom his very life, brain function, physical activity, feeling, and enjoyment of entertainments are impossible?

PARAMAHANSA-YOGANANDA-SECOND-COMING-OF-CHRIST-VOL.1, 585

Sri Swami Sivananda (1887-1963)

Real austerity consists of the control of the senses and the mind, not mortification of the body. The middle path between extreme asceticism and self-indulgence is beneficial. Fasting is external austerity; repentance and meditation are internal austerity.

TOWARDS PERFECTION

Parvati asked, "O venerable Lord! Which of the many rituals observed in Thy honour doth please Thee most?" The Lord replied, "The 14th night of the new moon, in the dark fortnight during the month of Phalgun, is my most favorite day. It is known as Shivaratri. My devotees give me greater happiness by mere fasting than by ceremonial baths and offerings of flowers, sweets and incense.

[SHIVARATRI BY SRI SWAMI SIVANANDA].

Sarvepalli Radhakrishnan (1888 –1975)

To attain heaven which is the higher level of understanding of being, one has to undergo inner growth, growth in wisdom and stature through prayer and fasting, through meditation and self-control ...

The Kingdom of Heaven is the highest state attainable by man. It is within us ... Our ordinary level of consciousness is not the highest form or the sole mode of experience possible to man. To get at the inner experience we must abstract from the outer. We must get away from the tumult of sense impressions, the riot of thoughts, the surgings of emotions, the throbs of desires.

[RELIGION, SCIENCE AND CULTURE, P. 14]

Anandamayi Ma (1896 –1982)

If you hanker after anything such as name, fame or position, God will bestow it on you, but you will not feel satisfied.

The Kingdom of God is a whole, and unless you are admitted to the whole of it you cannot remain content. He grants you just a little, only to keep your discontent alive, for without discontent there can be no progress ... He Himself kindles the sense of want in you by granting you a small thing, only to whet your appetite for a greater one. This is His method by which He urges you on...

The distress that is experienced burns to ashes all pleasure derived from worldly things. This is what is called 'tapasya' [austerity]. What obstructs one on the spiritual path bears within itself seeds of future suffering. Yet the heartache,[and] the anguish over the effects of these obstructions, are the beginning of an awakening to Consciousness."

[THE SRI ESSENTIAL ANANDAMAYI MA, P. 89]

David Simon, M.D. (1951-2012)

The fifth branch of yoga is known as pratyahara – a word that is traditionally translated as "control of the senses" or "sensory fasting." In our view, the essence of pratyahara is temporarily withdrawing from the world of intense, externally imposed stimulation so that we can tune into our subtle sensory experiences.

Yoga and Ayurveda recommend that we take time to disengage from the exterior world so that we can hear our inner voice more clearly. Meditation is a form of pratyahara since, in the space of restful awareness, we disengage from the outside environment. When the mind's attention is withdrawn from the sensory field, the senses naturally come to rest.

In a way, pratyahara can be seen as sensory fasting. The word pratyahara is comprised of the root prati meaning "away" and ahara meaning "food." If we fast for a period of time, the next meal we eat will usually be exceptionally delicious. Yoga suggests that the same concept applies to all our experiences in the world. If we take the time to withdraw from the world for a little while, we will find that our experiences are more vibrant.

[EXPLORING THE EIGHT LIMBS OF YOGA].

Deepak Chopra, M.D. (1946 -)

Fasting has traditionally been a part of many cultures and figures in most religions; our morning meal, for example, is called "breakfast" because there was once a fast to break. If fasting does prove to have a physiological benefit, this proof could be connected to the observation that fasting raises the level of growth hormone secreted by the pituitary.

CREATING HEALTH: HOW TO WAKE UP THE BODY'S INTELLIGENCE, P.95

Silence is the great teacher, and to learn its lessons you must pay attention to it. There is no substitute for the creative inspiration, knowledge, and stability that come from knowing how to contact your core of inner silence. The great Sufi poet Rumi wrote, "Only let the moving waters calm down, and the sun and moon will be reflected on the surface of your being."

[AGELESS BODY, TIMELESS MIND, P. 318].

Sadhguru Jaggi Vasudev (1957-)

It is important that you don't fast forcefully. If you observe the natural cycle of the body, there is something called a mandala. The mandala means that every 40 to 48 days, the system goes through a certain cycle. In every cycle, there are three days when your body does not need food. If you are conscious of how your body functions, you will become aware that on these days, your body does not need food. And without effort, you can go without food on that day.

[IS THERE ANY BENEFIT TO FASTING?]

So if you want to fast, first of all prepare the body by eating the right kind of foods. If it is a great torture when you hold back your urge to eat, you will only cause damage to the system. Maybe you are thinking of performing some kind of a feat "I did not eat for three days," and you want to go and tell that to the whole world. Please don't do such things. It is of no benefit to you. You will just make yourself weak, that is all.

[IS THERE ANY BENEFIT TO FASTING?]

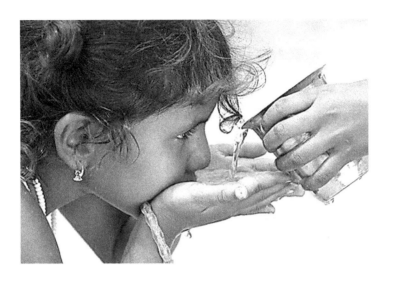

5

BUDDHIST SOURCES

5.1 Fasting in Buddhist Scripture

The Buddha (c 560BC – c 460BC) taught the "middle way." Regarding food, this means a path between extreme abstinence and depraved gluttony. Although the Buddha fasted under the Bodhi tree for 49 days, there is no Buddhist scripture (sutra) that requires fasting. In the three major Buddhist traditions, Vajrayana, Theravada and Mahayana, fasting is not advocated.

Nevertheless, based on their canon, spiritual authorities and individual practitioners have developed specific rules and customs that regulate eating and the practice of fasting. The objective is to develop discipline and self-control with moderation.

Unlike the ascetic mortification of Hinduism, the Buddhist fast is best described as restrained eating. For example, the fasting practice of *Nyungne* is widely practiced in Tibet.

5.2 Udana

To speak no ill, to injure not. To be restrained according to the precepts. To be temperate in food. To sleep secluded. To dwell on lofty thoughts, This is the law of the Buddha.

[UDANA MEGHIYA, 59].

Clinging, in bondage to desires, not seeing in bondage any fault, thus bound and fettered, never can they cross the flood so wide and mighty. Blinded are beings by their sense desires spread over them like a net; covered are they by the cloak of craving; by their heedless ways caught as a fish in the mouth of a funnel-net. Decrepitude and death they journey to, just as a sucking calf goes to its mother.

[UDANA 75-76].

5.3 Mahāsatipatthāna Sutta

And what, monks, is Right Awareness? Here, monks, a monk dwells ardent with awareness and constant thorough understanding of impermanence, "<u>observing body in body</u>, having removed craving and aversion towards the world [of mind and matter]; he dwells ardent with awareness and constant thorough understanding of impermanence, <u>observing sensations in sensations,</u> having removed craving and aversion towards the world [of mind and matter]; he dwells ardent with awareness and constant thorough understanding of impermanence, <u>observing mind in mind,</u> having removed craving and aversion towards the world [of mind and matter]; he dwells ardent with awareness and constant thorough understanding of impermanence, <u>observing mental contents in mental contents,</u> having removed craving and aversion towards the world [of mind and matter]. This, monks, is called Right Awareness.

[MAGGASACCANIDDESO (THE GREAT DISCOURSE ON THE ESTABLISHING OF AWARENESS)]

5.4 Dhammapada

Just as a storm throws down a weak tree, so does Mara (the Tempter) overpower the man who lives for the pursuit of pleasures, who is uncontrolled in his senses, immoderate in eating, indolent and dissipated.

[DHAMMAPADA: CH. 1, THE PAIRS].

Do not indulge in careless behavior. Do not be the friend of sensual pleasures. He who meditates attentively attains abundant joy.

[DHAMMAPADA 2:27].

Elusive and unreliable as it is, the wise man straightens out his restless, agitated mind, like a fletcher crafting an arrow. Trying to break out of the Tempter's control, one's mind writhes to and fro, like a fish pulled from its watery home onto dry ground. It is good to restrain one's mind, uncontrollable, fast-moving and following its own desires as it is. A disciplined mind leads to happiness.

[DHAMMAPADA 3:33-35].

He who lives looking for pleasures only, his senses uncontrolled, immoderate in his food, idle, and weak, Mara (the Tempter) will

*certainly overthrow him, as the wind throws down a weak tree. He
who lives without looking for pleasures, his senses well controlled,
moderate in his food, faithful and strong, him Mara will certainly
not overthrow, any more than the wind throws down a strong
mountain.*

[DHAMMAPADA V. 7-8].

*Men who have no riches, who live on recognized food, who have
perceived void and unconditioned freedom, their path is difficult to
understand, like that of birds in the air. He whose appetites are
stilled, who is not absorbed in enjoyment, who has perceived void
and unconditioned freedom, his path is difficult to understand, like
that of birds in the air.*

[DHAMMAPADA 7:92].

*Not nakedness, not platted hair, not dirt, not fasting, or lying on the
earth, not rubbing with dust, not sitting motionless, can purify a
mortal who has not overcome desires.*

[DHAMMAPADA 10.141].

*Restraint of the eyes is good. So is restraint of the ears.
Restraint of the nose is good, and so is restraint of the palate.
Restraint of the body is good. So is restraint of speech.
Restraint of mind is good, and so is restraint in everything.
The bhikkhu who is restrained in everything, is freed from all
suffering.*

[THE DHAMMAPADA, 360-1]

5.5 Bhaddāli Sutta

*So I have heard. At one time the Buddha was staying near
Sāvatthī in Jeta's Grove, Anāthapiṇḍika's monastery. There
the Buddha addressed the mendicants, "Mendicants!"*

"Venerable sir," they replied. The Buddha said this:

*"Mendicants, I eat my food in one sitting per day. Doing so,
I find that I'm healthy and well, nimble, strong, and living
comfortably. You too should eat your food in one sitting per
day. Doing so, you'll find that you're healthy and well, nimble,
strong, and living comfortably."*

*When he said this, Venerable Bhaddāli said to the Buddha,
"Sir, I'm not going to try to eat my food in one sitting per day.
For when eating once a day I might feel remorse and regret."*

*"Well then, Bhaddāli, eat one part of the meal in the place
where you're invited, and bring the rest back to eat. Eating
this way, too, you will sustain yourself."*

[MIDDLE DISCOURSES 65, WITH BHADDĀLI]

5.6 Latukikopama Sutta

Udāyī, these are the five kinds of sensual stimulation. What five? Sights known by the eye that are likable, desirable, agreeable, pleasant, sensual, and arousing. Sounds known by the ear ... Smells known by the nose ... Tastes known by the tongue ... Touches known by the body that are likable, desirable, agreeable, pleasant, sensual, and arousing. These are the five kinds of sensual stimulation.

The pleasure and happiness that arise from these five kinds of sensual stimulation is called sensual pleasure—a filthy, ordinary, ignoble pleasure. Such pleasure should not be cultivated or developed, but should be feared, I say.

Take a mendicant who, quite secluded from sensual pleasures, secluded from unskillful qualities, enters and remains in the first absorption ... second absorption ... third absorption ... fourth absorption.

This is called the pleasure of renunciation, the pleasure of seclusion, the pleasure of peace, the pleasure of awakening. Such pleasure should be cultivated and developed, and should not be feared, I say...

So, Udāyī, I even recommend giving up the dimension of neither perception nor non-perception. Do you see any fetter, large or small, that I don't recommend giving up?"

"No, sir."

[SIMILE OF THE QUAIL]

5.7 Cūlaassapura Sutta

And how does a mendicant practice in the way that is proper for an ascetic?

There are some mendicants who have given up covetousness, ill will, irritability, hostility, offensiveness, contempt, jealousy, stinginess, deviousness, deceit, bad desires, and wrong view. These stains, defects, and dregs of an ascetic are grounds for rebirth in places of loss, and are experienced in bad places. When they have given these up, they are practicing in the way that is proper for an ascetic, I say.

[THE SHORTER DISCOURSE AT ASSAPURA]

5.8 Ganakamoggallāna Sutta

When they guard their sense doors, the Realized One guides them further: 'Come, mendicant, eat in moderation. Reflect properly on the food that you eat: 'Not for fun, indulgence, adornment, or decoration, but only to sustain this body, to avoid harm, and to support spiritual practice. In this way, I shall put an end to old discomfort and not give rise to new discomfort, and I will live blamelessly and at ease.'

[MIDDLE DISCOURSES 107, WITH MOGGALLĀNA THE ACCOUNTANT

5.9 Additional Buddhist Sources

Mazu Daoyi (709–788)

To eat and drink is your natural right, to abstain from meat and wine is your chance for greater blessedness.

QUOTED IN THE ZEN EXPERIENCE.BY THOMAS HOOVER, CH. 6.

Huang Po His Yu (died 850)

FIRST, learn how to be entirely unreceptive to sensations arising from external forms, thereby purging your bodies of receptivity to externals.

THE ZEN TEACHINGS OF HUANG PO: ON THE TRANSMISSION OF MIND

Thich Nhat Hanh (1926 -)

Do we need to eat all the time, every day? I just finished a fourteen days fast, and I look fine. I even look better. You may think that I am a little bit thin, but I feel fine. By fasting, by not doing anything, by abandoning all projects, all desires, you allow your body to stop, to rest, to renew itself. And that is why during the time you are with us in Plum Village; try your best to learn the art of stopping, of resting.

... In fact, fasting is a very wonderful way of healing yourself. The most difficult disease you have may just be healed by fasting.

[RETURNING TO OUR TRUE HOME]

Sitting in meditation is nourishment for your spirit and nourishment for your body, as well.

[THE MIRACLE OF MINDFULNESS]

Venerable Master Chin Kung (1927–)

Likewise, when we practice adhering to the precepts, the most important point is to follow their fundamental spirit, "Do nothing that is bad: do everything that is good". "To do nothing that is bad" is directed toward us. This is a Theravada precept to develop self-discipline and is to be followed conscientiously. It is what the Chinese call "Attending to one's own moral wellbeing even while alone". When we practice self-discipline we need to remain true to the precepts, even when we are alone.

TO UNDERSTAND BUDDHISM, CH.5

Self-discipline cures our body, deep concentration cures our mind and wisdom cures our behavior. Therefore, a person who practices Buddhism is wise in thought, speech and behavior. So how could such a person be unhappy?

TO UNDERSTAND BUDDHISM, CH.6

Dalai Lama (14th) (1935 –)

It is felt that a disciplined mind leads to happiness and an undisciplined mind leads to suffering, and in fact, it is said that bringing about discipline within one's mind is the essence of the Buddha's teaching.

[THE ART OF HAPPINESS BY DALAI LAMA, P. 46]

The fasting practice known as nyungne, which involves eating only one meal on the first day and fasting completely on the second, is often done in conjunction with taking the eight Mahayana precepts ... Nyungne is an authentic and effective Buddhist practice employing the actions of our body, speech, and mind that has been enthusiastically followed in India, Tibet, and the surrounding regions for many centuries past, and which those who are interested can easily undertake wherever they are today.

[BUDDHIST FASTING PRACTICE: THE NYUNGNE METHOD OF THOUSAND-ARMED CHENREZIG BY WANGCHEN RINPOCHE, INTRODUCTION]

There are three types of fasting recognized by the Qur'an: ritual fasting, fasting as compensation or repentance, and ascetic fasting. While fasting after midday is one of the precepts of a monk in the Buddhist tradition, it is impressive that Islam has extended this restraint of the senses to all practitioners, especially during the holy month of Ramadan.

[HOW THE TOWARD A TRUE KINSHIP OF FAITHS: HOW THE WORLD'S RELIGIONS
CAN COME TOGETHER P. 84]

Rev. Heng Sure, Ph.D. (1949 -)

Laity who receive and observe the vows known as the Lay Bodhisattva Precepts stop eating at noon on six days of each month . . . The fasting observance is related to several liturgical practices observed on the six fasting days: they recite their precept codes, recite scriptures and increase their hours of meditation on those days.

[REV. HENG SURE, PH.D., ON FASTING FROM A BUDDHIST'S PERSPECTIVE].

Tsem Tulku Rinpoche (1965–2019)

In Buddhism, fasting is considered a method of purification. Theravadin monks fast every day after 12pm till the next sunrise. The Tibetan Buddhist practice of Nyungne, which includes holding strict vows and fasting, has been gaining increased attention in Buddhist centers across North America. Fasting in Buddhism is to develop control of one's attachments so the mind can be freed to develop higher awareness.... Basically to restrict one's body from the normal food intake is to develop discipline, awareness, self-control and even appreciation for all one has.

[FASTING BUDDHA]

Wangchen Rinpoche

A combination of the vow of fasting with deity visualization, prayer, mantra recitation, etc. has enormous benefit according to Nyungne leaching. Unlike ordinary fasting, Nyungne fasting is done with true enlightened motivation, and therefore the power of pure spiritual intention and action creates correct causes and conditions, which in turn will lead to correct results; that is, purification of negativity and accumulation of merit. The results will be temporary and ultimate benefits. Temporarily the benefits will be freedom from sickness, longevity, and a range of other benefits; ultimately there would be complete freedom from samsara and enlightenment.

[BUDDHIST FASTING PRACTICE: THE NYUNGNE METHOD OF THOUSAND-ARMED CHENREZIG , P. 202].

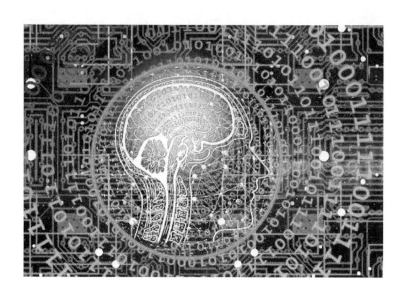

6

OTHER NOTABLE SOURCES

Can a mind engrossed in modern secular desires experience the far-reaching benefits of a spiritual fast? Can a heart immersed in fashionable worldly allurements recognize the profound significance of fasting? We often think, speak and behave in ways produced by our appetites:

Beware lest thou forget Jehovah thy God... lest, when thou hast eaten and art full, and hast built goodly houses, and dwelt therein; and when thy herds and thy flocks multiply, and thy silver and thy gold is multiplied, and all that thou hast is multiplied; then thy heart be lifted up, and thou forget Jehovah thy God, ... and lest thou say in thy heart, My power and the might of my hand hath gotten me this wealth.

[Deuteronomy 8:11-17 (ASV)].

Laozi (c.601–530BC)

But people like the side paths.

The courts are corrupt.

The fields are barren

The warehouses are empty

Officials wear fineries

Carry sharp swords

Fill up on drinks and food

Acquire excessive wealth

This is called robbery

It is not the Tao!

[TAO TE CHING]

Chuang Tzu (369–286 BC)

"You must fast!" said Confucius. "Do you know what I mean by fasting? It is not easy. But easy ways do not come from God."

[THE WAY OF CHUANG TZU, THOMAS MERTON]

The goal of fasting is inner unity. This means hearing, but not with the ear; hearing, but not with the understanding; hearing with the spirit, with your whole being. The hearing that is only in the ears is one thing. The hearing of the understanding is another. But the hearing of the spirit is not limited to any one faculty, to the ear, or to the mind. Hence it demands the emptiness of all the faculties. And when the faculties are empty, then the whole being listens. There is then a direct grasp of what is right there before you that can never be heard with the ear or understood with the mind. Fasting of the heart empties the faculties, frees you from limitation and from preoccupation. Fasting of the heart begets unity and freedom."

[THE WAY OF CHUANG TZU, BY THOMAS MERTON]

Acharya Amritchandra (c.10th – 11th century)

For the sake of strengthening the performance of daily meditation (sāmāyika), one must undertake fasting twice each lunar fortnight.

Free from all routine activities, and giving up attachment to own body, etc., one should commence fasting from mid-day prior to the day of fasting (the eighth and the fourteenth day of each lunar fortnight).

[PURUSHARTHA SIDDHYUPAYA (REALIZATION OF THE PURE SELF) (JAINA TEXT)]

Atahualpa, Inca XIII (c. 1502–1533)

Tell your captain [Pizarro] that I am keeping a fast, which will end tomorrow morning. I will then visit him, with my chieftains. In the meantime, let him occupy the public buildings on the square, and no other, till I come, when I will order what shall be done."

[W. H. PRESCOTT, HISTORY OF THE CONQUEST OF PERU: VOL. 1, P. 238]

Gurū Nānak (1469–1539)

I do not keep fasts, nor do I observe the month of Ramadaan. I serve only the One, who will protect me in the end. The One Lord, the Lord of the World, is my God Allah. He administers justice to both Hindus and Muslims.

[GURU GRANTH SAHIB JI, ANG 1136]

Let your mind be content, and be kind to all beings. In this way, your fast will be successful. Keep your wandering mind restrained in one place. Your mind and body shall become pure, chanting the Lord's Name. The Supreme Lord God is pervading amongst all.

(GURU GRANTH SAHIB JI, ANG 299)

Let all thy religion, the way of works, fasting, worship, and daily conduct Be this: that thou knowest not another but the Transcendent

SRI GURU GRANTH SAHIB, VOL. 1, P. 190

Thomas Jefferson (1743–1826)

We never repent of having eaten too little.

1825 LETTER TO JOHN SPEAR SMITH

We were under conviction of the necessity of arousing our people from the lethargy into which they had fallen as to passing events; and thought that the appointment of a day of general fasting and prayer would be most likely to call up and alarm their attention. No example of such a solemnity had existed since the days of our distresses in the war of 55. since which a new generation had grown up. With the help therefore of Rushworth, whom we rummaged over for the revolutionary precedents and forms of the Puritans of that day, preserved by him, we cooked up a resolution, somewhat modernizing their phrases, for appointing the 1st day of June, ..., for a day of fasting, humiliation and prayer, to implore heaven to avert from us the evils of civil war, to inspire us with firmness in support of our rights, and to turn the hearts of the King and parliament to moderation and justice.

THE PAPERS OF THOMAS JEFFERSON, VOLUME 1: 1760 TO 1776

Abraham Lincoln (1809–1865)

It behooves us then, to humble ourselves before the offended Power, to confess our national sins, and to pray for clemency and forgiveness.

Now, therefore, in compliance with the request, and fully concurring in the views of the Senate, I do, by this my proclamation, designate and set apart Thursday, the 30th. day of April, 1863, as a day of national humiliation, fasting and prayer. And I do hereby request all the People to abstain, on that day, from their ordinary secular pursuits, and to unite, at their several places of public worship and their respective homes, in keeping the day holy to the Lord, and devoted to the humble discharge of the religious duties proper to that solemn occasion.

PROCLAMATION APPOINTING A NATIONAL FAST DAY, MARCH 30, 1863

Henry Wadsworth Longfellow (1807–1882)

You shall hear how Hiawatha
Prayed and fasted in the forest,
Not for greater skill in hunting,
Not for greater craft in fishing,
Not for triumphs in the battle,
And renown among the warriors,
But for profit of the people,
For advantage of the nations...

First he built a lodge for fasting,
Built a wigwam in the forest,
By the shining Big-Sea-Water,
In the blithe and pleasant Spring-time,
In the Moon of Leaves he built it,
And, with dreams and visions many,
Seven whole days and nights he fasted.

THE SONG of HIAWATHA

Bahá'u'lláh (1817–1892)

*Hold ye fast unto His statutes and commandments, and be not
of those who, following their idle fancies and vain imaginings,
have clung to the standards fixed by their own selves, and
cast behind their backs the standards laid down by
God. Abstain from food and drink from sunrise to sundown,
and beware lest desire deprive you of this grace that is
appointed in the Book.*

[THE KITÁB-I-AQDAS, 17 (BAHA'I TEXT)].

William James (1842–1910)

Keep the faculty of effort alive in you by a little gratuitous exercise every day. That is, be systematically ascetic or heroic in little unnecessary points, do every day or two something for no other reason than that you would rather not do it, so that when the hour of dire need draws nigh, it may find you not unnerved and untrained to stand the test.

[THE PRINCIPLES OF PSYCHOLOGY, CH. 4, HABIT,].

[Our] normal waking consciousness, rational consciousness as we call it, is but one special type of consciousness, whilst all about it, parted from it by the filmiest of screens, there lie potential forms of consciousness entirely different. We may go through life without suspecting their existence; but apply the requisite stimulus, and at a touch they are there ... No account of the universe in its totality can be final which leaves these other forms of consciousness quite disregarded.

[THE VARIETIES OF RELIGIOUS EXPERIENCE, 308].

326 Fasting for God

Suffice it meanwhile that each of us literally chooses, by his ways of attending to things, what sort of a universe he shall appear to himself to inhabit.

[THE PRINCIPLES OF PSYCHOLOGY].

The feeling of the inward dignity of certain spiritual attitudes, as peace, serenity, simplicity, veracity; and of the essential vulgarity of others, as querulousness, anxiety, egoistic fussiness, etc.,—are quite inexplicable except by an innate preference of the more ideal attitude for its own pure sake. The nobler thing **tastes** *better, and that is all that we can say.*

[THE WILL TO BELIEVE, P. 120],

Arnold Ehret (1866–1922)

All miracles performed by saints at the so-called holy places have become rare forthe simple reason that, although much praying is done, not much fasting is adhered to. We don't have miracles any more because we have no more saints, no more blessed and healed by asceticism and fasting. The saints were radiant not by special grace but through divine healthy asceticism.

[RATIONAL FASTING: FOR PHYSICAL, MENTAL, AND SPIRITUAL REJUVENATION, P. 38].

Rudolf Steiner (1861–1925)

One's personality can be strengthened by training the will. One can, for example, say to oneself: Within five years I shall acquire a new habit and during that time I shall concentrate my whole will-power upon achieving it. When the will is trained in this way, for the sake of inner perfection, then one loosens, without ascetic practices, the soul-spiritual from the bodily nature. The first discovery, when such training of the will is undertaken for the sake of self-improvement, is that a continuous effort is needed. Every day something must be achieved inwardly. Often it is only a slight accomplishment but it must be pursued with iron determination and unwavering will.

[GUIDANCE IN ESOTERIC TRAINING, PP. 157-8].

We can ask ourselves if we do not make our bodies unfit for the execution of the intentions, aspirations and impulses of our lives if we become bound by and dependent upon our bodies through an unsuitable diet. Is it not possible to mold the body in such fashion that it turns into a progressively more suitable instrument for the impulses of our spiritual life? ... The wrong food can easily transform us into what we eat, but by permeating ourselves with knowledge of the spiritual life, we can strive to become free and independent. Then the food we eat will not hinder us from achieving the full potential of what we ... ought to be.

[PROBLEMS OF NUTRITION].

Henri Bergson (1859–1941)

*Fortunately, some are born with spiritual immune systems
that sooner or later give rejection to the illusory worldview
grafted upon them from birth through social conditioning.
They begin sensing that something is amiss, and start looking
for answers. Inner knowledge and anomalous outer
experiences show them a side of reality others are oblivious
to, and so begins the journey of awakening. Each step of the
journey is made by following the heart instead of the crowd,
and by choosing knowledge over veils of ignorance.*

[ATTRIBUTED TO HENRI BERGSON, ON INTUITION VS. INTELLECT].

Ernest Holmes (1887–1960)

Fasting and prayer often do bring our thought closer to Reality, not because of the fasting or the prayer, but because they open up greater fields of receptivity in our minds. If one wishes to embody an ideal and is willing to give up all else to attain it, then he is fasting and praying!

[THE SCIENCE OF MIND]

William Griffith Wilson (1895–1971)

It is easy to let up on the spiritual program of action and rest on our laurels. We are headed for trouble if we do, for alcohol is a subtle foe. We are not cured of alcoholism. What we really have is a daily reprieve contingent on the maintenance of our spiritual condition. Every day is a day when we must carry the vision of God's will into all of our activities. "How can I best serve Thee - Thy will (not mine) be done." These are thoughts which must go with us constantly. We can exercise our will power along this line all we wish. It is the proper use of the will.

[ALCOHOLICS ANONYMOUS, P.85]

Richard L. Veech, M.D., Ph.D. (c. 1936–)

Normally, our body converts carbohydrates into glucose for energy. However, when we use up our glucose, our body switches to ketonic energy.

During periods of food deprivation, our digestive system breaks down stored fatty acids and converts them into ketone bodies. These substitute for glucose as fuel for the brain. It can be argued that since ketone bodies are the only available alternative to glucose for the brain's energy, ketosis was a critical evolutionary development to provision man's hypertrophied brain while sparing muscle mass.

[KETONE BODIES, POTENTIAL THERAPEUTIC USES].

Ketones are part of our normal metabolism when we are starving. That's why they exist. If there is little food, so long as you have water you can live for at least 76 days, for much of that time with increased mental ability and physical energy. If you had to rely on glucose for energy you would be dead in six days.

[KETONES].

These data suggest a similar increase in metabolic efficiency in [the] human brain using ketoacids as the principal source of energy in place of glucose ... [G]iven the body of evidence already existing showing the therapeutic efficacy of ketone bodies in a variety of conditions ... ketone therapy seems warranted.

[KETONE BODIES, POTENTIAL THERAPEUTIC USES].

Rupert Sheldrake, Ph.D. (1942–)

The most powerful way to stimulate the secretion of natural growth hormones without ... undesirable side effects is by fasting. In one study, growth hormone secretion more than doubled over a five-day fasting period, and a study of a religious forty-day fast found that growth hormone levels increase more than tenfold without the use of any drugs all.

[WAYS TO GO BEYOND AND WHY THEY WORK: SPIRITUAL PRACTICES IN A SCIENTIFIC AGE, PP. 81-82]

Fasting is not in itself a spiritual experience, but is a practice that interrupts the normal habits of appetite and bodily desire. It creates a space in which spiritual realities can be more present. The decision to fast is taken with the intention of going beyond regular desires and habits. Fasting creates a mental and physical context in which other spiritual practices, like prayer and meditation, can be more effective.

[WAYS TO GO BEYOND AND WHY THEY WORK: SPIRITUAL PRACTICES IN A SCIENTIFIC AGE, P. 268]

Andrew Weil, M.D. (1942—)

Fasting owes its effectiveness to a basic fact of physiology. The digestive organs are the largest and bulkiest in the body, and their routine operations consume large amounts of energy. The simple act of not eating, or eating only simple foods, frees up much of that energy for the body to use in healing. Fasting means taking in nothing other than water (or water and herbal teas with no calories). Restricting yourself to liquids, fruit, or fruit juice is not fasting. These are special diets that have particular benefits but do not produce the same results as fasting

[NATURAL HEALTH, NATURAL MEDICINE: THE COMPLETE GUIDE TO WELLNESS AND SELF-CARE FOR OPTIMUM HEALTH]

Harold G. Koenig, M.D. (1951—)

The general principle here, which is supported by other Scriptures as well as several thousand years of religious practice by those of a wide variety of religious persuasion, is that fasting can be a means of attaining heightened spiritual awareness and empowerment for overcoming difficulties or fulfilling a difficult task. Fasting includes forgoing, for a period of time, food or other things that one might enjoy. Its benefits are gained through prayer, Scripture reading, and meditation during the fast. The denial of one's desires can prepare the way for a clearer perception of the presence and will of God.

DAVID B. BIEBEL, HAROLD G. KOENIG, NEW LIGHT ON DEPRESSION: HELP, HOPE, AND ANSWERS FOR THE DEPRESSED AND THOSE WHO LOVE THEM, P. 213.

Marianne Williamson (1952—)

The only way to break from your subconscious belief that eating is the source of your comfort is by building on your faith that God is the source of your comfort ... You can't break your dysfunctional habit of doing whatever the fear-mind commands except by building on your relationship with love. You must cultivate a passion for what you really, truly want. And what you really, truly want is love.

That is the meaning of discipleship, which obviously comes from the same root as the word discipline. Your problem is not lack of discipline, but rather misplaced discipline. Discipleship means disciplining yourself to serve the Divine.

[A COURSE IN WEIGHT LOSS, P. 190]

Joel Fuhrman, M.D. (1953–)

The unique nutritional adjustments that occur during a total fast, including the adaptation to ketone nutrition, apparently have long-term beneficial effects on brain function, improving psychological health as well as physical well-being. When EEG data and endocrine parameters are measured during and after fasting, it appears the homeostasis mechanism of the body significantly improves in the central nervous system.

FASTING AND EATING FOR HEALTH, PP. 198-199

The modern food and drug industry has converted a significant portion of the world's people to a new religion—a massive cult of pleasure seekers who consume coffee, cigarettes, soft drinks, candy, chocolate, alcohol, processed foods, fast foods, and concentrated dairy fat (cheese) in a self-indulgent orgy of destructive behavior. When the inevitable results of such bad habits appear— pain, suffering, sickness, and disease—the addicted cult members drag themselves to physicians and demand drugs to alleviate their pain, mask their symptoms, and cure their diseases. These revelers become so drunk on their addictive behavior and the accompanying addictive thinking that they can no longer tell the difference between health and health care.

EAT TO LIVE, P. 168

Jordan B. Peterson, Ph.D. (1962—)

Clear principles of discipline and punishment balance mercy and justice so that social development and psychological maturity can be optimally promoted. Clear rules and proper discipline help the child, and the family, and society establish, maintain, and expand the order that is all that protects us from chaos and the terrors of the underworld, where everything is uncertain, anxiety-provoking, hopeless and depressing.

12 RULES FOR LIFE: AN ANTIDOTE TO CHAOS P. 144].

If your life is not going well, perhaps it is your current knowledge that is insufficient, not life itself. Perhaps your value structure needs some serious retooling. Perhaps what you want is blinding you to what else could be. Perhaps you are holding on to your desires, in the present, so tightly that you cannot see anything else— even what you truly need.

[12 RULES FOR LIFE, P. 99].

There's a profound idea in the ancient Vedic texts ... the world, as perceived, is maya—appearance or illusion. This means, in part, that people are blinded by their desires ... You are blind, because of what you desire. Perhaps what you really need is right in front of your eyes, but you cannot see it because of what you are currently aiming for.

[12 RULES FOR LIFE, P. 98]

Satan first tempts the starving Christ to quell His hunger by transforming the desert rocks into bread. ...Christ responds to the first temptation by saying, "One does not live by bread alone, but by every word that proceeds from the mouth of God." ... [This] means that even under conditions of extreme privation, there are more important things than food. ...Bread is of little use to the man who has betrayed his soul, even if he is currently starving ... Gluttony, in the midst of moral desolation? That's the poorest and most miserable of feasts. ... [What] if we all chose instead of expedience to dine on the Word of God?

[12 RULES FOR LIFE, P. 182]

EPILOGUE

Fasting has always provided a spiritual refuge for piety and sanctity. However, consumerism and technology have infiltrated some of its spiritual boundaries. Ours may be the only civilization to adopt intermittent fasts merely for cosmetic purposes.

Nevertheless, amid therapeutic hype and faddish pseudo-science, fasting remains impregnable to modernization. In fact, the therapeutic and psychological benefits inherent in fasting provide a gateway into the spiritual, transcendent aspects of religious life. Often, what starts with profane motives rises to the level of intimate worship, reflecting our timeless pursuit of Divine awareness.

> *Today, especially in affluent societies, St. Augustine's warning is more timely than ever: 'Enter again into yourself.' Yes, we must enter again into ourselves, if we want to find ourselves. Not only our spiritual life is at stake, but indeed, our personal, family and social equilibrium, itself. One of the meanings of penitential fasting is to help us recover an interior life. Moderation, recollection and prayer go hand in hand.* [POPE JOHN PAUL II].

Distracted Minds

Clearly, today's hectic material existence clutters our thinking. We are constantly interrupted by recurring worldly desires and fleeting emotions. As a result, our distracted minds have little time to reflect on meaningful blurred fragments of transient realities.

> *There are days when the entire Jewish people [should] fast ... to arouse [their] hearts and initiate [them in] the paths of repentance. This will serve as a reminder of our wicked conduct and that of our ancestors, which resemble our present conduct and therefore brought these calamities upon them and upon us. By reminding ourselves of these matters, we will repent and improve [our*

conduct], as [Leviticus 26:40] states: "And they will confess their sin and the sin of their ancestors." [MISHNEH TORAH, SEFER ZEMANIM, TA'ANIYOT, CHAPTER FIVE HALACHA 1].

How do we make room in our lives for the Divine? Do we tools that can take us beyond our preoccupied, engrossed intellect, tools that can redirect our secular perspective and point our thoughts toward the Eternal.

Empty for God

Vacare Deo literally means "to be empty for God." This suggests that we should engage our mind in attending to our Creator. The quality of our life depends on the quality of our thoughts.

> *Consumerism, instead of satisfying needs, constantly creates new ones ... Everything seems necessary and urgent and one risks not even finding the time to be alone with oneself for a while ... St Augustine's warning is more timely than ever. "Enter again into yourself." Yes, we must enter again into ourselves if we want to find ourselves. Not only our spiritual life is at stake but indeed our personal, family and social equilibrium itself. [POPE JOHN PAUL II, SUNDAY ANGELUS - MARCH 10, 1996].*

The quotations in this book offer ample evidence that, throughout history, fasting has been an incomparable tool for sobering the intellect and promoting spiritual awareness. In a fasting mode, our mind becomes introspective, opening our consciousness to different frequencies, to different ways of listening and understanding.

When our shallow pleasures lose their appeal, when our hunger is for spiritual nourishment, and when our existence demands answers, then only Divine thoughts can satisfy. Spiritually sober, we abandon our arrogance, discard our fleeting illusions, and rush back to the Forgiver, the Merciful.

> *O humanity! Behold, We have created you all out of a male and a female, and have made you into nations and tribes, so that you might come to know one another. Verily, the noblest of you in the*

sight of God is the one who is most deeply conscious of Him. Surely, God is all-knowing, all-aware. [QURAN, 49:13 (ASAD)]

BIBLIOGRAPHY

Judaic Sources

- Babylonian Talmud: Berakoth 17, Atenebris Adsole. Retrieved 8 September 2019, from http://www.come-and-hear.com/berakoth/berakoth_17.html
- Ben Sira 34:26 - King James Version w/ Apocrypha (KJVA). (2019). Retrieved 8 September 2019, from https://www.biblestudytools.com/kjva/ben-sira/34-26.html
- Biblical Studies Press. (2006). *Holy Bible, New English Translation (NET)*. Spokane.
- Bonder, N. (1998). *The Kabbalah of Food* (p. 97). Boston: Shambhala.
- Buber, M., & Friedman, M. (2015). *Hasidism & modern man* (pp. 68, 69). Princeton & Oxford: Princeton University Press.
- Davies, N. (2011). The Jewish Retreat Centre- Our Interior Sanctuary (March 2011). Retrieved 9 September 2019, from https://jewishcontemplatives.blogspot.com/2011/03/jewish-retreat-centre-our-interior.html
- Fine, L. (1984). *Safed spirituality*. New York: Paulist Press.
- Full text of "The Apocalypse Of Elijah.pdf (PDFy mirror)." Retrieved 8 September 2019, from https://archive.org/stream/pdfy-8kXMoCqhZarIc0pj/The%20Apocalypse%20Of%20Elijah_djvu.txt
- Görg, P. (2011). *The desert fathers*. San Francisco, Calif: Ignatius Press.
- Holy Bible, King James Version (KJV). (1611). Retrieved 8 September 2019, from https://www.kingjamesbibleonline.org/Deuteronomy-Chapter-14/

- Holy Bible, The Complete Tanakh (Tanach) - (JPS) - The Jewish Bible with a Modern English Translation and Rashi's Commentary. Retrieved 8 September 2019, from https://www.chabad.org/library/bible_cdo/aid/63255/jewish/The-Bible-with-Rashi.htm

- Ignatius Press. (2005). *Holy Bible, Revised Standard Version (RSV).* San Francisco.

- Jewish New Testament Publications. (1998). *Holy Bible, Complete Jewish Bible (CJB).*

- Kook, A. (2010). Selected Quotes from Rabbi Kook. Retrieved 9 September 2019, from http://www.israelnationalnews.com/News/News.aspx/139091

- Kook, A., & Morrison, C. (2006). *Gold from the land of Israel* (p. 178). Jerusalem: Urim publ.

- Maimonides, M. The Rambam's Mishneh Torah. Retrieved 8 September 2019, from https://www.chabad.org/library/article_cdo/aid/682956/jewish/Mishneh-Torah.htm

- Maimonides, M. The Rambam's Mishneh Torah. Retrieved 8 September 2019, from https://www.chabad.org/library/article_cdo/aid/910345/jewish/Deot-Chapter-Five.htm#lt=primary

- Moore, G. (1927). *Judaism* (p. 265). Cambridge: Harvard Univ. Press.

- Philo Judaeus. Philo: On the Contemplative Life. Retrieved 9 September 2019, from http://www.earlyjewishwritings.com/text/philo/book34.html

- Philo Judaeus. Philo: On the Life of Moses, II. Retrieved 8 September 2019, from http://www.earlychristianwritings.com/yonge/book25.html

- Philo Judaeus. Philo: The Special Laws, I. Retrieved 8 September 2019, from http://www.earlychristianwritings.com/yonge/book27.html

- Pinchas Winston, R. (2002). Holy Sparks #3: Soul Food. Retrieved 9 September 2019, from https://www.aish.com/sp/k/48950471.html

- Saint Benedict Press. (2000). *Holy Bible, Douay-Rheims (DRB)*. Charlotte.

- Schneur Zalman, R. The Tanya. Retrieved 9 September 2019, from https://www.chabad.org/library/tanya/tanya_cdo/aid/1029225/jewish/Chapter-3.htm

- Scholem, G. (1973). *Sabbatai Ṣevi* (p. 293). London: Routledge & Kegan Paul.

- Shepherd, M. (2016). *Textuality and the Bible* (p. 39). Eugene: Wipf and Stock Publishers.

- Shimon bar Yochai, R. Heat Your Heart Out - The laws of kosher kitchenware teach us about sweetening judgments. Retrieved 9 September 2019, from https://www.chabad.org/kabbalah/article_cdo/aid/379621/jewish/Heat-Your-Heart-Out.htm

- Taanit 16a:1. Retrieved 8 September 2019, from https://www.sefaria.org/Taanit.16a.1?ven=Sefaria_Community_Translation&lang=bi

- The Apocalypse of Abraham. Retrieved 8 September 2019, from http://www.pseudepigrapha.com/pseudepigrapha/Apocalypse_of_Abraham.html

- The Book of the Apocalypse Of Baruch. Retrieved 8 September 2019, from http://www.pseudepigrapha.com/pseudepigrapha/2Baruch.html

- The Psalms of Solomon. Retrieved from http://www.goodnewsinc.net/othbooks/psalmsol.html

- The Testaments of the Twelve Patriarchs (Roberts-Donaldson). Retrieved 8 September 2019, from http://www.earlychristianwritings.com/text/patriarchs.html

- Tract Taanith: Chapter I. Retrieved 8 September 2019, from https://www.sacred-texts.com/jud/t04/taa06.htm

Christian Sources

- Ambrose, S., Liebeschuetz, J., & Hill, C. (2005). *Ambrose of Milan: Political letters and speeches* (p. 301). Liverpool: Liverpool University Press.

- Ante-Nicene Fathers, Vol II: The Pastor of Hermas: Similitude Fifth. Of True Fasting and Its Reward: Also of Purity of Body. Retrieved 9 September 2019, from https://www.sacred-texts.com/chr/ecf/002/0020027.htm

- Aquilina, M. (2000). *The Way of the Fathers: Praying with the Early Christians*. Huntington, Ind.: Our Sunday Visitor.

- Augustine, Outler, A., & Augustine. (2006). *Augustine*. Louisville: Westminster John Knox.

- Baab, L. (2006). *Fasting: Spiritual Freedom Beyond Our Appetites* (p. 30). InterVarsity Press.

- Baab, L. (2012). *Fasting: Spiritual Freedom Beyond Our Appetites*. InterVarsity Press.

- Barsanuphius, John, & Chryssavgis, J. (2006). *Letters* (p. 103). Washington, D.C.: Catholic University of America Press.

- Basil the Great. Homily on Fasting. Retrieved 9 September 2019, from https://georgianorthodoxchurch.wordpress.com/2012/03/08/saint-basil-the-greats-homily-on-fasting/

- Benson, E. Do Not Despair, Ensign, Oct 1986. Retrieved 13 October 2019, from https://www.churchofjesuschrist.org/study/ensign/1986/10/do-not-despair?lang=eng

- Bonhoeffer, D. (2014). *The cost of discipleship* (p. 169). New York: Touchstone.

- Bright, B. *Releasing God's power through fasting*. Retrieved 14 September 2019, from https://unityinchrist.com/prayer/print/fasting.htm

- Bunyan, J. (1814). *The pilgrim's progress from this world to that which is to come;... in three parts ...* (p. 384). London: Thomas Kelly.

- Butler, A. (1845). *The lives of the fathers, martyrs and other principal saints* (p. 25). Dublin: James Duffy.

- Calvin, J. (2008). *Institutes of the Christian religion* (p. 820). Peabody, MA: Hendrickson Publishers.

- Carty, C. (1994). *Padre Pio: The Stigmatist*. Charlotte: TAN Books.

- Cassian, J. (2019). The Training of a Monk and the Eight Deadly Sins, Book 5, Of the Spirit of Gluttony. Retrieved 12 September 2019, from http://www.thenazareneway.com/Institutes%20of%20John%20Cassian/book_5_the_spirit_of_gluttony.htm

- Cassian, J., Luibhéid, C., & Pichery, E. (1985). *Conferences* (p. 42). New York: Paulist Press.

- Channing, W. (1848). *The Works of William E. Channing* (p. 71). Boston: James Munroe.

- Chrysologus, P. Prayer, Fasting and Mercy by St. Peter Chrysologus, Early Church Father [Catholic Caucus]. Retrieved 12 September 2019, from http://www.freerepublic.com/focus/f-religion/2197020/posts

- Chrysostom, J. Fasting | Russian Orthodox Cathedral of St.John The Baptist. Retrieved 12 September 2019, from https://stjohndc.org/en/orthodoxy-foundation/lessons/fasting

- Clement, P. Clement, the Disciple of Peter: Two Epistles Concerning Virginity. Retrieved 9 September 2019, from http://passtheword.org/GOSPEL-Rediscovery/clement-concerningvirginity.htm

- Climacus, J. The Ladder of Divine Ascent. Retrieved 12 September 2019, from http://www.prudencetrue.com/images/TheLadderofDivineAscent.pdf

- de Vogüé, A. (1993). *To love fasting* (pp. 12, 116). Petersham, Mass.: Saint Bede's Publications.

- de Vogüé, A. (2019). Fr. Adalbert, de Vogüé, O.S.B. On Fasting. Retrieved 14 September 2019, from http://ldysinger.stjohnsem.edu/@texts2/1970_vog%C3%BC%C3%A9/02_love_fasting.htm

- Doctrine and Covenants. Chapter 34, 88:70–141. Retrieved 14 September 2019, from https://www.churchofjesuschrist.org/study/manual/doctrine-and-covenants-student-manual-2017/chapter-34-doctrine-and-covenants-88-70-141?lang=eng

- Du Bois, W., & Zuckerman, P. (2000). *Du Bois on religion* (pp. 24-25). Walnut Creek: Altamira Press.

- Eckhart, M. (2014). *Meister Eckhart's sermons* (p. 51). [Place of publication not identified]: Wyatt North Publishing.

- Eckhart, M., & Inge, W. (2015). *Light, Life, and Love*. London: Aeterna Press.

- Eckhart, M., Pfeiffer, F., & Evans, C. (1924). *Meister Eckhart, vol. 2* (p. 19). London: J.M. Watkins.

- Eckhart, M., Pfeiffer, F., & Evans, C. (1924). *Meister Eckhart, Volume 1* (p. 19). London: J.M. Watkins.

- Eddy, M. (1891). *Science and health* (pp. 16, 321). North Charleston, SC: Jazzybee Verlag.

- Eddy, M. (1913). *The first church of christ, scientist and miscellany* (pp. 339-340). Boston, Mass: Trustees under the Will of Mary Baker Eddy.

- Edwards, J. (2017). *The Works of Jonathan Edwards: Volume I* (p. 67). Woodstock, Ontario: Devoted Publishing.

- Elliot, E. (2006). *Discipline* (p. 46). Grand Rapids, MI: Fleming H. Revell.

- Finney, C. (1876). *Memoirs of Rev. Charles G. Finney* (p. 35). Bedford, MA: Applewood Books.

- Foster, R. (1988). *Celebration of discipline* (p. 47). New York: HarperOne.

- Finney, C. National Fast Day by Charles G. Finney from "The Oberlin Evangelist." Retrieved 13 October 2019, from https://www.whatsaiththescripture.com/Voice/Oberlin_1841/OE1841.National.Fast.Day.html

- Foster, R. *Freedom of Simplicity* (pp. 164-65). New York: Harper One.

- Fox, G. (1694). *A journal or historical account of the life, travels, sufferings ... of that ancient, eminent and faithful servant of Jesus Christ, George Fox.* (p. 376). London: Northcott, Thomas.

- Francis, P., Spadaro, A., Sherry, M., & Lombardi, F. (2016). *Encountering truth: meeting God in the everyday*. New York: Crown Publishing Group.

- Gleanings from Orthodox Christian Authors & the Holy Fathers - fasting. Retrieved 9 September 2019, from http://www.orthodox.net/gleanings/fasting.html

- Haase, A. (2008). *Coming home to your true self* (p. 108). Downers Grove, Ill.: IVP Books.

- Hall, F. (2016). *Glorified Fasting: The ABC of Fasting*. Ravenio Books.

- Hallesby, O. (1975). *Prayer* (p. 113). Minneapolis,: Augsburg Pub. House.

- Henry, M., & Scott, T. (1833). *A commentary upon the Holy Bible, from Henry and Scott* (p. 109). London: The Religious Tract Society.

- Irenaeus of Lyons, Fragments (Roberts-Donaldson translation). Retrieved 9 September 2019, from http://www.earlychristianwritings.com/text/irenaeus-fragments.html

- Jerome, S., Schaff, P., & Wace, H. (1893). *A select library of the Nicene and post-Nicene fathers of the Christian church, vol vi, St. Jerome* (p. 402). New York: Christian literature Co.

- Keating, T. (2012). *Invitation to love* (p. 105). London: Bloomsbury.

- Keating, T. (2014). *The human condition*. New York: Paulist Press.

- Keller, D. (2005). *Oasis of wisdom* (p. 148). Collegeville, Minn.: Liturgical Press.

- King, M., & Carson, C. (1998). *The autobiography of Martin Luther King, Jr.* (p. 70). New York: Warner Books, Inc.

- Knox, J. (1886). *The liturgy of John Knox* (p. 172). Glasgow: Hamilton, Adams & Company.

- Lake, K. (1913). *The Apostolic fathers* (p. 155). London: W. Heinemann.

- Lama, D., & Tutu, D. (2016). *The Book of Joy: Lasting Happiness in a Changing World.* [Place of publication not identified]: Penguin Publishing Group.

- Lewis, C. (1942). *The Problem of Pain* (p. 100). London: Geoffrey Bles.

- Lewis, C. (1998). *Mere Christianity* (p. 32). New York: Harper One.

- Lewis, C. (2001). *The screwtape letters* (p. 87). Harper One.

- Lewis, C., & Hooper, W. (2014). *God in the dock* (pp. 42-43). Grand Rapids, Cambridge: Wm. B. Eerdmans Publishing.

- Lippmann, W. (1982). *A preface to morals* (p. 161). New Brunswick: Transaction Publishers.

- Lloyd-Jones, D. (1961). *Studies in the Sermon on the mount* (p. 38). Grand Rapids: William B. Eerdmans Publishing Company.

- Luther, M. (2012). *Treatise on Good Works.* Authentic Media Limited.

- Luther, M., & Plass, E. (1959). *What Luther says* (p. 507). Saint Louis, Mo: Concordia Publ. House.

- Merton, T. (1999). *The seven storey mountain* (p. 148). London: Harcourt.

- Merton, T. (2010). *Seasons of celebration* (p. 113). New York: Farrar, Straus and Giroux.

- Mother Teresa. (2019). Her own words. Retrieved 13 September 2019, from https://www.motherteresa.org/her-own-words.html

- Mother Teresa of Calcutta, & Benenate, B. (2010). *In the Heart of the World: Thoughts, Stories and Prayers* (p. 10). Navato, CA: New World Library.

- Murray, A. (1885). *With Christ in the school of prayer* (p. 96). London: Fleming H, Revell Company.

- Murray, A. (1998). *Andrew Murray on prayer*. New Kensington, PA: Whitaker House.

- Murray, A. (2002). *Teach me to pray* (p. 89). Minneapolis: Bethany House.

- NPNF1-09. St. Chrysostom: On the Priesthood; Ascetic Treatises; Select Homilies and Letters; Homilies on the Statutes - Christian Classics Ethereal Library. (2019). Retrieved 10 September 2019, from http://www.ccel.org/ccel/schaff/npnf109.xix.v.html#xix.v-Page_358

- Origen, & Barkley, G. (2010). *Origen* (p. 206). Wash. D.C.: Catholic Univ. of America Pr.

- Ortberg, J. (2009). *Love beyond reason*. Grand Rapids: Zondervan.

- Ortberg, J. (2009). *The life you've always wanted: spiritual disciplines for ordinary people*. Grand Rapids: Zondervan.

- Ortberg, J., & Rubin, S. (2010). *The me I want to be: Becoming God's best version of you* (p. 50). Grand Rapids, MI: Zondervan.

- Ortberg, J., Harney, K., & Harney, S. (2010). *Teaching the heart of the Old Testament* (p. 141). Grand Rapids, Mich.: Zondervan.

- Philo Judaeus. On the Contemplative Life. Retrieved 9 September 2019, from http://www.earlyjewishwritings.com/text/philo/book34.html

- Piper, J. (2013). *A Hunger For God: Desiring God Through Fasting And Prayer* (pp. 21-22, 55). Wheaton, IL: Crossway.

- Polycarp to the Philippians (Lightfoot translation). Retrieved 9 September 2019, from http://www.earlychristianwritings.com/text/polycarp-lightfoot.html

- Pope Benedict XVI. (2009). Message of His Holiness Benedict XVI for Lent 2009. Retrieved 13 September 2019, from http://w2.vatican.va/content/benedict-xvi/en/messages/lent/documents/hf_ben-xvi_mes_20081211_lent-2009.html

- Pope Benedict XVI. (2011). General Audience of 9 March 2011: Ash Wednesday |. Retrieved 13 September 2019, from http://w2.vatican.va/content/benedict-xvi/en/audiences/2011/documents/hf_ben-xvi_aud_20110309.html

- Pope Clement XIII. On the Spiritual Advantages in Fasting - Papal Encyclicals. Retrieved 13 September 2019, from https://www.papalencyclicals.net/clem13/c13appet.htm

- Pope Gregory I. (1990). *Be Friends of God: Spiritual Reading from Gregory the Great* (p. 86). Cowley Publications.

- Pope John Paul II. (1966). Penitential Fasting Is Therapy for the Soul | EWTN. Retrieved 13 September 2019, from https://www.ewtn.com/catholicism/library/penitential-fasting-is-therapy-for-the-soul-8769

- Pope John Paul II. (1995). Encyclical Letter of Pope John Paul II - Evangelium Vitae. Retrieved 13 September 2019, from https://www.priestsforlife.org/magisterium/evtext.htm

- Pope Leo. Church Fathers: Sermon 12 (Leo the Great). Retrieved 12 September 2019, from http://www.newadvent.org/fathers/360312.htm

- Pope Paul VI. (1966). Paenitemini (February 17, 1966) | On Fast and Abstinence. Retrieved 13 September 2019, from http://w2.vatican.va/content/paul-vi/en/apost_constitutions/documents/hf_p-vi_apc_19660217_paenitemini.html

- Pope Pius XII. (1953). Christus Dominus - Papal Encyclicals. Retrieved 13 September 2019, from https://www.papalencyclicals.net/pius12/p12chdom.htm

- Pope Shenouda III. (1997). *The spirituality of fasting* (p. 58). .: Dar El Tebaa El Kawmia.

- Prudence Allen, S. Formation in an Electronic Age. Retrieved 14 September 2019, from https://www.catholicculture.org/culture/library/view.cfm?recnum=6693

- Russell, C. (2014). *Expanded Biblical comments, 1879-1916*. Chicago, Ill.: Chicago Bible Students.

- Ryan, F. (2019). Give your fasting two wings, Fr. Thomas Ryan. Retrieved 14 September 2019, from https://www.paulist.org/the-conversation/give-your-fasting-two-wings/

- Ryan, T. (2005). *The sacred art of fasting* (pp. 163-164). Woodstock, Vt.: SkyLight Paths Pub.

- Ryan, T. (2006). Fasting: A Fresh Look. Retrieved 14 September 2019, from https://www.americamagazine.org/issue/563/article/fasting-fresh-look

- Ryan, T. (2014). Give Your Fasting Two Wings. Retrieved 12 September 2019, from http://www.tomryancsp.org/news_Fasting-TwoWings.htm

- Singletary, M. (2014). *The 21-day financial fast*. Grand Rapids: Zondervan.

- Smith, H. (1956). *The God of All Comfort* (p. 145). Chicago: Moody Publishers.

- SMITH, J. (1948). *History of the Church of Jesus Christ of Latter Day Saints,* vol 7 (p. 413). Salt Lake City, Utah: Deseret Book Company.

- Smith, J., & Smith, H. (1911). *History of the Church of Jesus Christ of Latter Day Saints, 1873-1890* (p. 91). Lamoni, Iowa: Reorganized Church of Jesus Christ of Latter Day Saints.

- St Francis. The Rule of St Francis - 1223. Retrieved 12 September 2019, from http://www.thenazareneway.com/rule_of_st_francis.html

- St. Alphonsus de Liguori. (2016). *The Saint Alphonsus de Liguori Collection*. London: Catholic Way Publishing.

- St. Ambrose. (2015). *The Letters of Saint Ambrose, Bishop of Milan*. Oxford: Aeterna Press.

- St. Augustine, Boulding, M., & Rotelle, J. (2000). *Expositions of the Psalms* (p. 263). Hyde Park, NY: New City Press.

- St. Augustine. (2012). *On Christian Doctrine* (p. 8). Mineola: Dover Publications.

- St. Augustine. Fasting, Prayer, Charity for the Gift of Peace | EWTN. Retrieved 12 September 2019, from https://www.ewtn.com/catholicism/library/fasting-prayer-charity-for-the-gift-of-peace-9829

- St. Benedict. ~ Holy Rule of St. Benedict: Chapters 1-5 ~. Retrieved 12 September 2019, from http://www.holyrule.com/part1.htm

- St. Catherine of Siena. (2007). *Dialogue of St. Catherine of Siena* (p. 168). New York: Cosimo.

- St. Chrysostom. NPNF1-09. St. Chrysostom: On the Priesthood; Ascetic Treatises; Select Homilies and Letters; Homilies on the Statutes - Christian Classics Ethereal Library. Retrieved 12 September 2019, from http://www.ccel.org/ccel/schaff/npnf109.xix.v.html#xix.v-Page_358

- St. Francis de Sales. (1987). *The sermons of St. Francis de Sales for Lent given in 1622*. Rockford, Ill.: Tan Books.

- St. Francis de Sales. (2016). *An introduction to a devout life*. Ignatius Press.

- St. Gregory I. (2007). *The book of pastoral rule* (p. 137). Crestwood, N.Y.: St. Vladimir's Seminary Press.

- St. Hildegard, Baird, J., & Ehrman, R. (2004). *The letters of Hildegard of Bingen* (p. 107). New York: Oxford University Press.

- St. Justin Martyr. Saint Justin Martyr: First Apology (Roberts-Donaldson). Retrieved 9 September 2019, from http://www.earlychristianwritings.com/text/justinmartyr-firstapology.html

- St. Teresa of Avila. (2000). *The Way of Perfection: A Study Edition* (p. 62). Washington, D.C.: ICS Publications.

- St. Thérèse of Lisieux. (2010). *The Story of a Soul: The Autobiography of the Little Flower*. Huntington: TAN Books.

- St. Thomas Aquinas, Parker, J., Rivington, J., & Rivington, J. (1842). *Catena aurea* (p. 615). Oxford: John Henry Parker.

- St. Thomas More. (1847). *A Dialogue of comfort against tribulation* (p. 101). London: Charles Dolman.

- Tertullian, On Fasting (Roberts-Donaldson, translator). Retrieved 9 September 2019, from http://www.earlychristianwritings.com/text/tertullian33.html

- The Shepherd of Hermas (Roberts-Donaldson translation). Retrieved 9 September 2019, from http://www.earlychristianwritings.com/text/shepherd.html

- Thomas a Kempis. (1907). *Meditations, with prayers, on the life and loving-kindnesses of our Lord and Saviour, Jesus Christ. Of the Incarnation of Christ to his passion.* (p. 114). London: Kegan Paul Trench Trubner & Co.

- Thomas À Kempis. (1940). *The imitation or following of Christ.* Milwaukee: The Bruce Publishing Company.

- Thurman, H. (2019). *Deep is the Hunger*. Papamoa Press.

- Tolstoy, L. (1902). *The novels and other works of Lyof N. Tolstoï* (p. 547). New York: C. Scribner's Sons.

- Tyndale, W., & Frith, J. (1831). *The works of William Tyndale* (p. 127). London: Ebenezer Palmer.

- Underhill, E. (1920). *The essentials of mysticism, and other essays* (p. 15). New York: E.P. Dutton & Co.

- Vogué, A. (1991). *Asceticism today* (pp. 121-122). Petersham, MA: St. Bede's Publications.

- Vogüé, A. (1994). *To love fasting* (pp. 116, 121). Petersham, Mass.: Saint Bede's Publications.

- Wallis, A., & Gregory, S. (1968). *God's chosen fast* (pp. 9, 48, 55). Fort Washington, PA: CLC.

- Ward, B. (1997). *The wisdom of the Desert Fathers* (p. 29). Spencer, MA: Cistercian Publications by arrangement with SLG Press, Fairacres, Oxford.

- Ward, B. (2003). *The wisdom of the Desert Fathers, saying of the early Christian monks* (p. 27). London, New York: Penguin.

- Wesley, J. (1825). *Sermons on several occasions* (p. 348). London: j. Kershaw.

- Wesley, J. (1827). *The Journal of the Rev. John Wesley* (p. 104). London: J. Kershaw.

- Wesley, J. (1844). *Sermons on several occasions* (p. 249). New York, NY: G. Lane & C. B. Tippett.

- Wesley, J., & Emory, J. (1833). *The works of the Reverend John Wesley, A.M* (p. 25). New York: B. Waugh and T. Mason, for the Methodist Episcopal Church, J. Collord, printer.

- White, E. Counsels on Diet and Foods. Retrieved 14 September 2019, from https://m.egwwritings.org/en/book/384.1487

- Willard, D. Spiritual Disciplines, Spiritual Formation and the Restoration of the Soul |. Retrieved 14 September 2019, from http://www.dwillard.org/articles/individual/spiritual-disciplines-spiritual-formation-and-the-restoration-of-the-soul

- Williams, J. (2013). *Spirit Cure: A History of Pentecostal Healing* (p. 69). New York: Oxford University Press.

- Zondervan Bible Publishers. (1996). *Holy Bible, New International Version (NIV)*. Grand Rapids, Mich.

- Zwingli, U. (1912). *The Latin works and the correspondence of Huldreich Zwingli together with selections from his German works* (p. 87). New York: G. P. Putman's Sons.

Islamic Sources

- Abd al-Qādir al-Jīlānī, & Bayrak, T. (1992). *The secret of secrets* (pp. 82-83). Cambridge: The Islamic Text Society.

- Al-Asi, M. (2008). The ascendant Qur'an: realigning man to the divine power culture vol. 2 (pp. 218-219). Toronto: Institute of Contemporary Islamic Thought.

- Al Mansour, K. (1992). Welcome to Islam (p. 200). [Place of publication not identified]: First African Arabian Press.

- Al-Bukhārī, M., & Khan, M. (1983). *Ṣaḥīḥ al-Bukhārī* (6th ed., pp. 64-122). Lahore: Kazi Publications.

- Al-Ghazali, A., & Farah, C. (1992). *Abstinence in Islam* (pp. 59-60). Minneapolis: Bibliotheca Islamica.

- Al-Ghazali. Revival of Religious Learnings-Ihya Ulum-Id-Din, Vol. 1 - Chapter 6. Retrieved 16 September 2019,

- Al-Ghazzali. Al-Ghazzali's The Mysteries of Fasting. Retrieved 16 September 2019, from http://sunnah.org/ibadaat/fasting/ramadan2.html

- Al-Hilali, M., & Khan, M. (1993). *Interpretation of the meanings of the noble Quran in the English language* (pp. 581-582). Riyadh, Saudi Arabia: Maktaba Dur-us=Salam.

- An-Nawawī. (2010). *Al-Nawawi forty hadiths and commentary*. New York: Arabic Virtual Translation Center.

- Asad, M. (1984). *Message of the Qur'an*. Gibraltar: Dar Al-Andalus.

- Chishti, M. Israr e Haqiqi by Moinuddin Chishti. Retrieved 16 September 2019, from https://archive.org/details/IsrarEHaqiqiByMoinuddinChishti/page/n7

- Darqāwī, M. (1979). *The Darqawi way: letters from the shaykh to the fuqara* (pp. 109-110). Ann Arbor: Diwan Press, 1979.

- Gülen, F. (2005). *Questions & Answers about Islam, Volume 2* (p. 22). Somerset, NJ: Tughra Books.

- Hoffman, V. (1995). Eating and Fasting for God in Sufi Tradition. *Journal Of The American Academy Of Religion, LXIII*(3), 465-484. doi: 10.1093/jaarel/lxiii.3.465

- Ibn 'Abdi'l-Barr. Kitab al-Kafi - fasting. Retrieved 16 September 2019, from http://bewley.virtualave.net/kafifast.html

- Ibn al-'Arabi, M. Selections from al-Futuhat al-Makkiyya, Ch. 71, On the Secrets of Fasting. Retrieved 16 September 2019, from http://bewley.virtualave.net/fut71a.html

- Ibn al-'Arabī., M., & Hirtenstein, S. (2008). *The Four Pillars of Spiritual Transformation: The Adornment of the Spirituality Transformed (Ḥilyat Al-abdāl) (Mystical Treatises of Muhyiddin Ibn 'Arabi)* (p. 34). Oxford: ANQA Publishing.

- Ibn Bāz, '., 'Uṯaymīn, M., Ibn Ǧibrīn, '., & Musnad, M. (2002). *Fatawa regarding fasting & Zakah*. Riyadh [etc.]: Darussalam.

- Ibn Mas'ood, '. 'Abdullaah Ibn Mas'ood (d. 32) – Quotes From The Salaf. Retrieved 16 September 2019, from https://quotesfromthesalaf.wordpress.com/category/search-via-name/abdullaah-ibn-masood-d-32/

- Ibn Qayyim al-Jawzīyah, M., & Al-Akili, M. (1993). Natural healing with tibb medicine, medicine of the Prophet (p. 254). Philadelphia: Pearl Publishing House.

- Ibn Taymiyyah. Ibn Taymiyyah on Night Prayers in Ramadhan – 11 or 20 Rak'ahs? |. Retrieved 15 September 2019, from http://www.bakkah.net/en/taymiyyah-night-prayers-ramadhan-11-20-rakahs.htm#more-1175

- Imam Ali Ibn Abi Talib. Various Sayings of Imam Ali Ibn Abi Talib (as). Retrieved 16 September 2019, from https://www.al-islam.org/articles/various-sayings-imam-ali-ibn-abi-talib

- Imam Ja'far Al-Sadiq. (1989). *The lantern of the path* (pp. 53, 92, 93). Dorsey, U.K.: Element Books.

- Iqbāl, M., & Nicholson, R. (1920). *The secrets of the self* (pp. 75, 78). London: Macmillan.

- Izz Ibn `Abd Al-Salam. (2012). "Fasting repels bad Thoughts". Retrieved 16 September 2019, from https://daralnicosia.wordpress.com/2012/07/11/part-3-fasting-repels-bad-thoughts/from http://www.ghazali.org/ihya/english/ihya-vol1-C6.htm

- Khan, I. The sufi message of Hazrat Inayat Khan, Vol. 6, The alchemy of happiness. Retrieved 15 September 2019, from http://hazrat-inayat-khan.org/php/views.php?h1=26&h2=23

- Malcolm X. (2011). *The end of white world supremacy*. [S.l.]: Skyhorse.

- Malcolm X, & Perry, B. (1989). *Malcolm X* (p. 43). New York: Pathfinder.

- Mālik ibn Anas, & Bewley, A. (1989). *Al-Muwatta of Imam Malik ibn Anas* (p. 117). London & New York: Kegan Paul.

- Menk, I. (2017). Mufti Menk's Quotes. Retrieved 15 September 2019, from https://storiesformuslimkids.wordpress.com/mufti-menks-quotes/

- Mohammed, W. (1976). Bilalian News Article 9-24-76: Ramadan. Retrieved 15 September 2019, from http://www.newafricaradio.com/articles/9-24-76.html

- Muhammad, E. (1967). *How to eat to live, Volume 2* (pp. 42, 49, 52,). Secretarius MEMPS Publications.

- Naqub Al -Misri, A., & Keller, N. (1997). *Reliance of the traveler*. Beltsville, MD: Amana Publications.

- Nasr, S. (2010). *Islamic life and thought* (p. 214). Kuala Lumpur: Islamic Book Trust.

- Nurbakhsh, D. Sufism Today - The Nimatullahi Sufi Order. Retrieved 15 September 2019, from https://www.nimatullahi.org/sufism-today/

- Nursi, S. Letters - Google Play. Retrieved 15 September 2019, from https://play.google.com/books/reader?id=9cSxDAAAQBAJ&printsec=frontcover&pg=GBS.PA1

- Pickthall, M. (1977). *The meaning of the glorious Qur'an.* Mecca & New York: Muslim World League - Rabita.

- Prophet Muhammad. Prophet's Sermon on the Month of Ramadan - IslamiCity. Retrieved 16 September 2019, from https://www.islamicity.org/6084

- Rumi, J. (2015). Mystical Poems of Rumi, pp.201-250 - Text Version | FlipHTML5. Retrieved 16 September 2019, from http://fliphtml5.com/gjfk/mldr/basic/201-250

- Rumi, J. The Song of the Reed. Retrieved 16 September 2019, from http://www.dar-al-masnavi.org/n-I-0001.html

- Rumi., J., & Chittick, W. (1983). *The Sufi path of love* (p. 157). Albany: State University of New York Press.

- Schuon, F., & Nasr, S. (2005). *The Essential Frithjof Schuon* (p. 235). Bloomington, Ind.: World Wisdom.

- Shakir, Z. (2017). Ramadan: Time to Get Real. Retrieved 15 September 2019, from https://medium.com/@zaytunacollege/ramadan-time-to-get-real-e788084ab014

- Smith, M. (1984). *Rābi'a the mystic and her fellow saints in Islām* (p. 29). Cambridge: Cambridge Univ. Press.

- Taqī 'Uthmāni, M. (2012). What Fasting Demands From Us | Mufti Taqi Uthmani. Retrieved 15 September 2019, from https://muslimmatters.org/2019/05/02/what-fasting-demands-from-us-mufti-taqi/

- 'Umar ibn Al-Khattab. Umar's Instructions on the First Night of Ramadan - Sayings of the Salaf. Retrieved 16 September 2019, from https://www.sayingsofthesalaf.net/umars-instructions-on-the-first-night-of-ramadan/

- 'Umar, A. Ten Statements From The Salaf On Love & Hate For Allah's Sake - Ummah.com - Muslim Forum. Retrieved 16 September 2019, from https://www.ummah.com/forum/forum/islam/general-islamic-topics/175106-ten-statements-from-the-salaf-on-love-hate-for-allah-s-sake

- Yusuf Ali, A. (1996). *The meaning of the Holy Qur'ān* (8th ed.). Beltsville, MD: Amana.

- Zarabozo, J. (2008). *Commentary on the Forty Hadith of al-Nawawi*. Denver, CO: Al-Basheer Company for Publications and Translations.

Hindu Sources

- Anandamayi, S., Lipski, A., & Fitzgerald, J. (2007). The essential Śrī Ānandamayī Mā: Life and Teachings of a 20th Century Indian Saint (p. 89). Bloomington: World Wisdom.

- Aurobindo, S. (2016). Bases of Yoga: Art of living. Kolkata, India: editionNEXT.

- Aurobindo, S., & Ghose, A. (1949). Essays on the Gita (9th ed., p. 489). Pondicherry: SriAurobindoAshram Publication.

- Badarayana. The Vedanta Sutras of Badarayana: Third Adhyâya. Fourth Pâda.: III, 4, 26. Retrieved 30 August 2019, from https://www.sacred-texts.com/hin/sbe38/sbe38235.htm

- Balaram Swami, K. (1986). Ekādaśī, the day of Lord Hari. Bombay: Bhaktivedanta Institute.

- Bhagavad Gita - Chapter 5 - The Yoga of Renunciation of Action. Retrieved 30 August 2019, from http://www.santosha.com/philosophy/gita-chapter5.html

- Bhagavad Gita, The Song of God – Swami Mukundananda. Retrieved 30 August 2019, from https://www.holy-bhagavad-gita.org/chapter/2/verse/66

- Bhagvad Gita. (2014). *Srimad bhagvad gita.* [Place of publication not identified]: Manish Chandra Prabhakar.

- Bhaktivedanta Swami Prabhupada, A. (1982). *Srimad Bhagavatam.* Los Angeles: Bhaktivedanta Book Trust.

- Bhāgavata Purāṇa, ŚB 11.8.21. Retrieved 22 September 2019, from https://vedabase.io/en/library/sb/11/8/21/

- Chopra, D. (1991). *Creating Health: How to Wake Up the Body's Intelligence* (p. 95). Boston: Houghton Mifflin Co.

- Chopra, D. (1993). *Ageless body, timeless mind* (p. 318). New York: Three Rivers Press.

- Dr S.P. Bhagat. (2016). Linga Purana. Lulu.

- Gandhi, M. (1927). Fasting | The Story of My Experiments with Truth | Gandhi Autobiography. Retrieved 30 August 2019, from https://www.mkgandhi.org/autobio/chap108.htm

- Gandhi, M. (1947). India of My Dreams. Retrieved 30 August 2019, from https://www.mkgandhi.org/ebks/India-Dreams.pdf

- Gandhi, M. (1962). Fasting and Prayer | Mahatma Gandhi: Selected Letters-II. Retrieved 30 August 2019, from https://www.mkgandhi.org/Selected%20Letters/sl_56.htm

- Manu, Haughton, G., Jones, W., & Percival, P. (1863). *Manava Dharma Sástra or the Institutes of Manu according to the gloss of Kulluka* (4th ed., p. 27). Madras: Asian Educational Services.

- Melpathur Narayana Bhattathiri. Complete Narayaneeyam. Retrieved 30 August 2019, from https://sanskritdocuments.org/sites/completenarayaneeyam/new-sansMainIndexV1.htm?conn=B

- Muller, F. (1884). Sacred books of the east, volume 15, (p. 179). Oxford: Clarendon Press.

- Narasimha Sthuthi of Prahlada. Narasimha Sthuthi of Prahlada - Hindupedia, the Hindu Encyclopedia. Retrieved 30 August 2019, from http://www.hindupedia.com/en/Narasimha_Sthuthi_of_Prahlada

- Narayana, S. (1882). The Sikshâ-Patrî of the Svâmi-Nârâya.na Sect. Retrieved 30 August 2019, from https://www.sacred-texts.com/journals/jras/ns14-24.htm

- Olivelle, P. (1998). The Early Upanishads: Annotated Text and Translation (p. 125). Oxford: Oxford University Press.

- Patanjali. Patanjali Yoga Sutra - Major Works in Vedic Philosophy. Retrieved 30 August 2019, from http://www.shankaracharya.org/patanjali_yoga_sutras.php

- Radhakrishnan, S. (1989). *Essays on religion, science & culture* (p. 14). Delhi: Orient Paperbacks.

- Ramanathan, A. Sannyasa Upanishad. Retrieved 22 September 2019, from http://www.advaita.it/library/sannyasa.htm

- Roy, P. (1965). The Mahabharata of Krishna-Dwaipayana Vyasa (2nd ed., p. 434). Calcutta: Oriental Publ.

- Sadhguru Jaggi Vasudev e. Is There Any Benefit to Fasting?. Retrieved 30 August 2019, from https://isha.sadhguru.org/au/en/wisdom/article/is-there-any-benefit-to-fasting?gclid=CjwKCAjwpuXpBRAAEiwAyRRPgUIgorD1ejSmbQ8uu1-e1jYnEXVTFE65ot2CLnMTrgWN7LAIf429LhoCTFUQAvD_BwE

- Shankaracharya, A. (1958). The Saundarya Lahari OR Flood Of Beauty. Retrieved 30 August 2019, from https://archive.org/details/TheSaundaryaLahariORFloodOfBeautyW.NormanBrown/page/n69

- Simon, D. (2016). A New Look at Yoga: Exploring the Eight Limbs of Yoga. Retrieved 30 August 2019, from http://web.archive.org/web/20160804113613/http:/www.chopra.com:80/files/Agni/davidsimon-anewlookatyoga.pdf

- Sivananda, S. Towards Perfection. Retrieved 22 September 2019, from http://sivanandaonline.org/public_html/?cmd=displaysection&section_id=964

- Sivananda, S. The Significance and Observance of Mahasivaratri. Retrieved 30 August 2019, from http://sivanandaonline.org/newsupdates/the-significance-and-observance-of-mahasivaratri/

- Swananda, S. (1989). *Complete works of Swami Vivekananda*. Calcutta: Advaita Ashrama.

- The Mahabharata, Book 3: Vana Parva: Markandeya-Samasya Parva: Section CLXLIX. Retrieved 30 August 2019, from https://www.sacred-texts.com/hin/m03/m03199.htm

- Vishnu Dharmothara Purana. Apamarjana Stotram. Retrieved 30 August 2019, from http://www.shastras.com/vishnu-stotras/apamarjana-stotram/

- Vyāsa, V. Margashirsha-Shukla Ekadasi. Retrieved 30 August 2019, from http://www.krishnapath.org/Ekadashi/Ekadashi_Stories/2.%20Margashirsha-Shukla%20Ekadasi.pdf

- Vyāsa, V. The Devi Bhagavatam: The Eleventh Book: Chapter 24. Retrieved 30 August 2019, from http://www.sacred-texts.com/hin/db/bk11ch24.htm

- Walters, J. (2004). *Conversations with Yogananda*. Nevada City, CA: Crystal Clarity Publishers.

- Yogananda, P. (2004). *The Second Coming of Christ* (p. 585). Los Angeles, Calif.: Self-Realization Fellowship.

Buddhist Sources

- Bhaddāli Sutta, Middle Discourses 47, The Inquirer. Retrieved 21 September 2019, from https://suttacentral.net/mn47/en/sujato

- Buddha, G. (2002). *The Dhammapada, translated by Friedrich Max Müller.* Woodstock, VT: SkyLight Paths Publishing.

- Chin Kung, M. To Understand Buddhism, Venerable Master Chin Kung. Retrieved 21 September 2019, from http://www.amtb.tw/e-bud/understanding_budd.html

- Cūlaassapura Sutta. Middle Discourses 40 The Shorter Discourse at Assapura. Retrieved 29 August 2019, from https://suttacentral.net/mn40/en/sujato

- Ganakamoggallāna Sutta. (2019). Middle Discourses 107, With Moggallāna the Accountant. Retrieved 29 August 2019, from https://suttacentral.net/mn107/en/sujato

- Hanh, T. (2013). Returning to Our True Home. Retrieved 29 August 2019, from https://plumvillage.org/transcriptions/returning-to-our-true-home/

- Hanh, T. (2016). *The miracle of mindfulness, gift edition* (p. 42). Boston, Mass.: Beacon Press.

- Hoover, T. (1980). The zen experience. Scarborough, Ont.: New American Library.

- Huang Po His Yun. (2016). Zen Teachings Of Huang Po. [Place of publication not identified]: Pickle Partners Publishing.

- Lama, D. (1998). *The art of happiness by the Dalai Lama and Howard Cutler* (p. 46). New York: Riverhead Books.

- Lama, D. (2011). *Toward a true kinship of faiths: How the World's Religions Can Come Together* (p. 84). New York: Three Rivers Press.

- Latukikopama Sutta. Middle Discourses 66 The Simile of the Quail. Retrieved 29 August 2019, from https://suttacentral.net/mn66/en/sujato

- Mahāsatipatthāna Sutta. The Great Discourse on the Establishing of Awareness. Retrieved 29 August 2019, from https://www.tipitaka.org/stp-pali-eng-parallel#25

- Rinpoche, W. (2009). *Buddhist Fasting Practice*. Lanham: Snow Lion Publications.

- Sure, Ph.D., R. A Buddhist Perspective on Fasting. Retrieved 29 August 2019, from http://www.urbandharma.org/udharma9/fasting.html

- Udana Meghiya. Full text of "The Udāna, or, The solemn utterances of the Buddha." Retrieved 30 August 2019, from http://www.archive.org/stream/cu31924022980472/cu31924022980472_djvu.txt

- Udana. Full text of "The Book of the discipline : (Vinaya-Pitaka)." Retrieved 29 August 2019, from http://www.archive.org/stream/bookofdiscipline08hornuoft/bookofdiscipline08hornuoft_djvu.txt

Other Notable Sources

- Amṛtacandra, & Jain, V. (2012). *Sri Amritchandra Suri's Puruṣārthasiddhyupāya (Purushartha siddhyupaya)* (p. 98). Dehradun: Vikalp Printers.

- Bahá'u'lláh. (2019). The Kitáb-i-Aqdas | Bahá'í Reference Library. Retrieved 29 August 2019, from https://www.bahai.org/library/authoritative-texts/bahaullah/kitab-i-aqdas/1#763968510

- Bahá'u'lláh. (2019). The Importance of Obligatory Prayer and Fasting. Retrieved 29 August 2019, from http://bahai-library.com/pdf/compilations/prayer_fasting.pdf

- Bergson, H. (2019). Quote by Henri Bergson. Retrieved 21 September 2019, from https://www.goodreads.com/quotes/875145-fortunately-some-are-born-with-spiritual-immune-systems-that-sooner

- Biebel, D., & Koenig, H. (2004). New Light on Depression: Help, Hope, and Answers for the Depressed and Those Who Love Them (p. 213). Grand Rapids, Mich.: Zondervan.

- Bill W (William Griffith Wilson). (2011). Alcoholics Anonymous: The Big Book (p. 82). Mineola, NY: IXIA Press (Dover).

- Ehret, A. (2016). Rational fasting. Dobbs Ferry, NY: Ehret Literautre Pub. Co.

- Ehret, A. (1971). Rational fasting: a scientific method of fasting your way to health (p. 38). New York: Benedict Lust Publications.

- Fuhrman, J. (2011). Eat to live. New York: Little, Brown.

- Fuhrman, J. (1995). Fasting and eating for health: A medical doctor's program for conquering disease (pp. 198-199). New York: St. Martin's Press.

- Fuhrman, J. (2011). The Cure for the American Diet: Nutrient Density. Retrieved 6 October 2019, from https://www.huffpost.com/entry/the-cure-for-the-american_b_695474?guccounter=1

- Holmes, E. (1998). The science of mind. New York: Penguin Publishing Group.

- James, W. (1950). *The Principles of Psychology, Volume 1* (p. 424). Courier Corporation.

- James, W. (1985). *The varieties of religious experience* (p. 308). Cambridge, Mass.: Harvard University Press.

- James, W. (2007). *The principles of psychology* (p. 126). New York: Cosimo.

- Jefferson, T., & Boyd, J. (2018). The Papers of Thomas Jefferson, Volume 1 (p. 106). Princeton: Princeton University Press.

- L. Veech, Britton Chance, Yoshihiro, R. (2001). Ketone Bodies, Potential Therapeutic Uses. *IUBMB Life (International Union Of Biochemistry And Molecular Biology: Life)*, *51*(4), 241-247. doi: 10.1080/152165401753311780

- Laozi., Lin, D., & Surya Das. (2006). *Tao te ching* (p. 107). Woodstock, Vt.: SkyLight Paths Pub.

- Lincoln, A. (1863). Abraham Lincoln's Proclamation Appointing a National Fast Day. Retrieved 29 August 2019, from http://www.abrahamlincolnonline.org/lincoln/speeches/fast.htm

- Longfellow, H. Longfellow: The Song of Hiawatha,. Retrieved 26 September 2019, from https://www.hwlongfellow.org/poems_poem.php?pid=279

- Merton, T. (2010). *The Way of Chuang Tzu (Second Edition)* (2nd ed.). New York: New Directions.

- Nanak, G. Ang 1136 of Guru Granth Sahib Ji - SikhiToTheMax. Retrieved 23 September 2019, from https://www.sikhitothemax.org/ang?ang=1136&source=G

- Peterson, J. (2018). *12 rules for life* (pp. 98-99, 144, 182). Canada: Random House.

- Sheldrake, R. (2019). Ways To Go Beyond and Why They Work (pp. 81-82, 268). Rhinebeck, NY: Monkfish Book Publishing, Co.

- Singh, G. (1960). Sri Guru Granth Sahib, Vol 1 (1st ed., pp. 208, 190). New Delhi: Allied Publishers.

- Steiner, R. (2008). An esoteric cosmology: evolution, christ & modern spirituality. [United States]: SteinerBooks.

- Steiner, R. (1909). Lecture: Problems of Nutrition. Retrieved 29 August 2019, from https://wn.rsarchive.org/Lectures/19090108p01.html

- Steiner, R. (1998). *Guidance in esoteric training* (3rd ed., pp. 157-158). Forest Row: Rudolf Steiner Press.

- Veech, R. (2017). Dr Richard L Veech. Retrieved 29 August 2019, from https://www.openfuture.biz/expertise/RichardVeech.html

- Weil, A. (2004). *Natural health, natural medicine.* Boston [Mass.]: Houghton Mifflin.

- Williamson, M. (2010). *A Course In Weight Loss* (p. 190). Hay House Publishing.

-

-